The Moscow KREMLIN

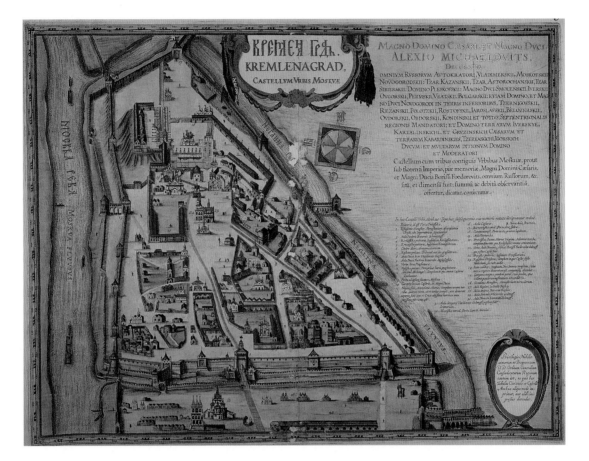

Kremlenagrad. Early 1600s plan. First published by H. Garritts in Amsterdam in 1813

The Moscow KREMLIN

English Edition

Having passed through the gates, you find yourself in
the Kremlin, amidst the most splendid assemblage of
palaces, churches and monasteries that you can only
picture in your imagination. They do not resemble any
style that we know: this is the Russian, Moscow style.
There is no other architecture on earth that would be
more free, singular and independent of rules—in a
word, more romantic—and capable of carrying out its
riotous whims with such a soar of fancy.

THÉOPHILE GAUTIER
A Journey to Russia. Paris, 1867

ART-RODNIK • *Moscow* • 2001

Text by
I. F. POLININA, I. A. RODIMTSEVA

Design by
V. Ya. CHERNIYEVSKY
L. V. DENISENKO

Photos by
N. N. RAKHMANOV

Translated from the Russian by
M. V. NIKOLSKY

ISBN 5–88896–066–7

Printed by NEOGRAFIA, Slovakia

Introduction

The Moscow Kremlin is a unique monument of the history of culture and an outstanding masterpiece of architecture and art.

The Moscow Kremlin was the centre of the formation of a single Russian state and the arena of numerous dramatic and glorious events. It has taken quite a few centuries for the architectural ensemble of the Kremlin, which is noted for its rare beauty and singularity of design, to take shape. It is by right called a stone chronicle reaching back to ancient times.

The first "records" in that chronicle were made by Prince Yuri Dolgoruky (Long-Armed), who owned Moscow in 1147; at the time it covered an area that was only part of the present-day Kremlin grounds. Burnt down by the Mongol-Tatars in 1218, Moscow rose anew from the ashes and continued to grow. The new walls of oak built around the Kremlin by Grand Duke Ivan Kalita ("Money-bags") by 1340 now protected the capital of a principality that comprised most of the Russian lands. It was also then that the first Cathedral of the Dormition, a small single-domed church, was built in the Kremlin.

The white-stone Kremlin walls erected in 1366-1367 were a challenge to the powerful Mongol empire. It was from the Kremlin that a unified Russian army led by Grand Duke Dmitry Donskoi of Moscow marched against the Mongol-Tatars, and his victory in the Battle of Kulikovo in 1380 marked the beginning of Russia's liberation from the foreign yoke. The walls built in the reign of Ivan III in the late 15th century became a symbol of the final overthrow of that yoke.

Having become the sovereign head of a powerful independent state, Ivan III launched grand-scale construction in the Kremlin: in addition to its fortress walls and towers a grand Palace of Facets, a new Cathedral of the Dormition, the Cathedrals of Archangel Michael and the Annunciation, the Church of the Deposition of the Virgin's Robe, and the Ivan the Great Bell Tower were built. This resulted in forming the architectural ensemble of Cathedral Square, which was then bounded on its southern side by the building of the Treasury Yard where the grand duke's riches were kept.

One of the major landmarks in the history of Russia was the adoption by Ivan IV of the title of a tsar: he was crowned tsar at the Kremlin Cathedral of the Dormition in 1547. It was also that year that the first mention of the Armoury, a depository of royal treasures, was made in the chronicles. In the reign of Ivan IV the Russian state began to press its former overlords, the successors of the Mongol-Tatars, which found expression in the construction of the Cathedral of the Protecting Veil on the Moat (also known as the Cathedral of St. Vassily the Blessed), the world-famous monument of Russian architecture, next to the Spasskiye (Saviour's) Gates known as the Frolovskiye (St. Florus') Gates at the time. The cathedral was built in commemoration of the victory over the Kazan Khanate.

The bitter struggle for national independence waged by the Russian people in the early 17th century was completed with the liberation of Kremlin from the followers of a foreign tsar, the son of the Polish king, in 1612. The country revived within an amazingly short period of time: it was in 1625 that a superstructure was added on top of the Spasskaya Tower and it acquired its present-day slim silhouette absolutely untypical of fortifications.

In the subsequent decades such buildings as the Terem Palace with Palace Churches and the Poteshny Palace were added to the architectural ensemble of the Kremlin. The Patriarch's Palace was completely rebuilt.

When a new capital, St. Petersburg, was built in the period of Peter the Great, Moscow remained a major centre of state administration and quite a few office buildings were concentrated in the Kremlin. They included the Treasury Yard, government office buildings dating from 1591 and 1673, the Arsenal, and, finally, the unsurpassed masterpiece by Matvei Kazakov known as the Senate (1776-1787), which is now the residence of the President of the Russian Federation.

The war of 1812 was a sore trial for Russia. Napoleon even succeeded in capturing Moscow for a short time. When retreating, the French blew up some of the Kremlin buildings and towers, which were restored after the Russian army entered Paris.

1. *The construction of the Kremlin walls and towers on its side facing the Great Posad (merchants' and artisans' quarter). Miniature from the 16th-century* Illuminated Chronicles

2. *Procession at the Spasskiye Gates in Red Square. Miniature from the book* Election of the Great Sovereign Tsar and Grand Duke Mikhail Feodorovich *to the Throne. 1672-1673*

In 1818, Alexander II, an emperor who abolished serfdom and a monarch who carried out reforms that filled the sails of the Russian state with fresh wind, was born in the Kremlin.

In the reign of Nicholas I, the Grand Kremlin Palace, a veritable monument of the grandeur of imperial Russia, was built in the Kremlin.

In March 1918, Moscow once again became the capital of Russia and the Kremlin,

4

4. *Empress Catherine the Great on Mono-makh's Throne in the Cathedral of the Dormition on the day of her coronation. Engraving from Empress Catherine the Great's coronation album*

5. *The proclaiming of the manifesto on the coronation of Emperor Nicholas I in Red Square in Moscow. Engraving from the 1828 coronation album*

6. *Emperor Alexander II on the Krasnoye Porch on the day of his coronation. From Emperor Alexander II's coronation album*

Red Square in the historic Victory Parade, casting the routed enemy's standards at the foot of the Mausoleum.

It is for quite a few centuries now that the Kremlin has been the centre and symbol of the Russian state. Only the finest Russian and foreign architects, who have created and preserved its historical and architectural complex that has no parallel anywhere in Europe, were always invited to carry out construction work in it. The Moscow Kremlin, including all of its structures built between the 15th and 20th centuries, has been included by UNESCO in its World Heritage List, a list of cultural sites and natural areas of outstanding value.

3. *Crowning Mikhail Feodorovich tsar in the Moscow Kremlin's Cathedral of the Dormition. Miniature from the book* Election of the Great Sovereign Tsar and Grand Duke Mikhail Feodorovich to the Throne. *1672-1673*

the seat of the government, which did not leave it even in 1941 when the Nazi army was at the approaches to Moscow and it would have taken enemy warplanes 10 minutes to reach Red Square, where Joseph Stalin addressed troops arrayed for a traditional parade to mark the anniversary of the October 1917 revolution on November 7, 1941. Less than four years passed and soldiers who had defeated Nazi Germany marched through

5

6

7

THE KREMLIN WALLS AND TOWERS

More than eight hundred years ago an ancient fortress that marked the beginning of the city of Moscow was built on high Borovitsky Hill. The approaches to the fortress on the south were protected by the Moskva River and on the west, by the Neglinnaya River. In the reign of Grand Duke Ivan Kalita the early wooden fortifications were replaced with oak walls and towers. In the days of Grand Duke Dmitry Donskoi the Kremlin was built of white stone. Its present-day walls and towers were erected in the 1480s and 1490s, in the reign of Ivan III, when Italian architects carried out reconstruction of the Kremlin on a grand scale. The construction of its unassailable walls and towers was completed in 1495, and it was also then that the area of the Kremlin was extended to its present size.

The Kremlin walls surrounding Borovitsky Hill span a total of 2,235 metres, stretching along the Moskva River, the Alexandrovsky Gardens and Red Square. The walls are from 3.5 to 6.5 metres thick and from 5 to 19 metres high depending on the terrain. In all, there are 19 towers in the Kremlin walls built along their perimeter and still another one that used to be a bridgehead watchtower.

The walls and towers were built according to all the rules of military art. On top of the walls there is a battle platform, up to 4.5 metres wide, protected by merlons with narrow embrasures.

The builders erected two cylindrical towers and one tower with walls divided into 16 sides at the corners of the Kremlin, which is triangular in plan, and rectangular towers on the perimeter of the walls. There were wells

7. *The Moscow Kremlin. A view from the Beklemishevskaya Tower*

8. *The Konstantino-Yeleninskaya, Nabatnaya and Spasskaya Towers*

9. *The Tsarskaya, Nabatnaya and Konstantino-Yeleninskaya Towers*

10. *The ruby star on top of the Spasskaya Tower*

inside the corner towers. Out of the six bartizans in front of gate towers only the Kutafya Tower built at the entrance to Troitskiye Gates in 1516 has survived to this day. The tall stone hip roofs on all the towers except the Nikolskaya Tower were built at the end of the 17th century. The hip roofs of the Spasskaya, Nikolskaya, Borovitskaya and Troitskaya Towers were topped with double-headed eagles, the state emblem of the Russian Empire. In 1935, five-pointed stars decorated with semiprecious stones were mounted in their place and then, two years later, these were replaced with glowing stars of ruby glass and a fifth star was mounted on the Vodovzvodnaya Tower. Each star weighs more than a ton and has a span of 3 to 3.75 metres.

One of the most beautiful Kremlin towers is the Spasskaya Tower built by the architect Pietro Antonio Solari of Milan in 1491. Until

9

gates and foreign ambassadors were met here.

In 1624-1625, the octagonal multitiered stone turret which now surmounts the rectangular part of the Spasskaya Tower was built under the direction of Bazhen Ogurtsov and Christopher Halloway. At the time Halloway mounted a clock with chimes on the tower one tier lower than its present-day clock (the first mention of a clock on the Spasskaya Tower dates back to 1585). Halloway's clock

11. *The Beklemi-shevskaya Tower*

11

10

1658 it was known as the Frolovskaya (St. Florus') Tower and then it was renamed the Spasskaya (Saviour's) Tower in honour of the Smolensk Icon of the Saviour placed above its gateway. This ten-storied tower adorned with white-stone carving is more than 67 metres high. In the 16th-17th centuries, the Spasskiye Gates served as the royal entrance into the Kremlin. Ceremonial processions led by the Patriarch of All Russia passed through these

rather soon went out of order and, on the orders of Peter the Great, was replaced with a new one that served until 1737.

The clock we see now—the famous Kremlin Chimes—acquired its present-day appearance and capability of playing music after its complete overhaul carried out by the Brothers Butenop firm in 1851-1852. The clock movement takes up three stories and is driven by three weights, each weighing 160 to 224 kilograms. The total weight of the clock is about 25 tons. The clock-faces installed on the four sides of the tower are more than 6 metres in diameter. The hour hand is just a little less than 3 metres long and the minute hand, 3.28 metres. Simultaneously with the Spasskaya Tower, another gate tower, the Nikolskaya (St. Nicholas') Tower, was laid down. It takes its name

14

13

12. *The southern wall of the Kremlin. A view from the Vodovzvodnaya Tower*

13. *The Tainitskaya Tower*

14. *The Konstantino-Yeleninskaya Tower*

from the icon of St. Nicholas that was mounted above its gates.

There is documentary evidence that this tower also had a clock. The octagonal turret crowned with a tall spire in the pseudo-Gothic style was built on top of the tower in 1816-1817. Rising next to the building of the Arsenal is a corner tower, built in 1492, with walls divided into 16 sides. This formidable defensive structure with walls that are four metres thick conceals a well filled with crystal-clear spring water, which is still in existence today. The tower was given its present name, the Corner Arsenal Tower, after the Arsenal was built next to it on the Kremlin grounds in the 18th century.

The Troitskaya (Trinity) Tower is the tallest among the Kremlin towers facing the Alexandrovsky Gardens. On its side facing the garden the tower is over 76 metres in height (80 metres to the top of the star). Built in 1495-1499, it was named after the *podvorye* (representation) of the Trinity-St. Sergy Monastery situated next to it in the Kremlin. In 1685, a multitiered superstructure with Gothic pointed arches and turrets with weather vanes was added to the tower. The next one after the Troitskaya Tower is the Komendantskaya (Commandant's) Tower. At one time, the commandant of Moscow took up residence in the Kremlin's Poteshny Palace situated behind this tower. Rising next to the building of the Armoury is the Oruzheinaya (Armoury) Tower.

The next gate tower was named the Borovitskaya Tower after the *bor* (pine forest) that once covered the south-western slope of Kremlin Hill (also known as Borovitsky Hill). It was used as an entrance to the service part of the tsar's residence, for the royal stables and grain and fodder storehouses were situated next to the Borovitskiye Gates. The next,

corner tower is situated on the bank of the Moskva River. In the first half of the 17th century, water elevating pumps and tanks that supplied water from the Moskva River to the Kremlin's royal palace were installed in this tower. This was the first water supply system with a water tower in the city. It was then that the tower was given its name, meaning Water Tower. In 1812, the tower was blown up by the retreating troops of Napoleon and later

15. *The Kutafya Tower. The Troitsky Bridge and the Troitskaya Tower*

16. *The eastern wall of the Kremlin. A view of the Senatskaya and Nikolskaya Towers*

situated near the present-day Moskvoretsky Bridge. It was named after Boyar Beklemishev, whose manor was located in the Kremlin near the tower.

Situated next to the Beklemishevskaya Tower is the Konstantino-Yeleninskaya (Sts. Constantine's and Helen's) Tower built in 1490 on the spot where a tower of the white-stone Kremlin dating from the reign of Grand Duke Dmitry Donskoi used to stand. It was

17. *The Srednyaya Arsenalnaya Tower*

18. *The Nikolskaya Tower. Details of the decor*

on it was restored under the supervision of the noted architect Osip Beauvais.

The towers situated on the Kremlin side facing the Moskva River include the Blagoveshchenskaya (Annunciation) Tower and the Tainitskaya Tower (Tower of Secrets) built by Antonio Fryazin in 1485. The Tainitskaya Tower had a secret well hidden inside it and a secret underground passage to the Moskva River to be used in case of a siege. The next

three towers (the First and Second Nameless Towers and the Petrovskaya Tower) were pulled down together with the Tainitskaya Tower in the days of Catherine the Great during preparations for the construction of an enormous Kremlin palace after the plans of Vassily Bazhenov. Later on they were rebuilt to old drawings with some minor alterations. Of particular importance as a defensive structure was the corner Beklemishevskaya Tower

through that tower that he entered the Kremlin after the victory in the historic Battle of Kulikovo. The tower was named after the Church of Sts. Constantine and Helen that stood nearby inside the Kremlin.

Closer to Red Square stands the relatively low Nabatnaya (Tocsin) Tower whose bell gave warning signals in case of fires or major events in the city. In 1771, during a popular unrest in Moscow known as the plague rebellion, the insurgent citizens sounded the tocsin calling the people to the Kremlin. After the rebellion was put down the tocsin was taken down and exiled to Siberia. Between the Nabatnaya and Spasskaya Towers there is a small turret placed on the wall known as the Tsarskaya (Tsar's) Tower. The height of the tower, including the weather vane, is less than 17 metres. At one time, the alarm bells of the fire department were hung it.

CATHEDRAL SQUARE

Cathedral Square is the Kremlin's main square and one of the oldest squares in Moscow. A number of outstanding monuments of Old Russian architecture are situated here. The Cathedrals of the Dormition, the Annunciation and the Archangel Michael, the Church of the Deposition of the Virgin's Robe, the ensemble of the Ivan the Great Bell Tower, the Palace of Facets and the Patriarch's Palace form a unique architectural complex.

Cathedral Square has witnessed numerous historic events in the life of the Russian state. Solemn processions on the days of major church feasts and great ceremonies of crowning tsars and emperors were held here. It was from Cathedral Square that foreign ambassadors entered the royal palace.

23. *Cathedral Square*

24. *A view of the Krasnoye Porch and the Ivan the Great Bell Tower*

25. *The domes of the Cathedrals of the Annunciation, the Archangel Michael and the Dormition and of the Ivan the Great Bell Tower*

impression of the strikingly harmonious, solemn and imposing look of this building.

The Cathedral of the Dormition embodied the idea of unity of the Russian land and expressed the desire of the Moscow princes to emphasise and affirm the might of the centralised state which was then in the process of formation.

The classic proportions of the building, its five mighty domes, smooth walls, the regular rhythm of its arcaded portals, windows and *zakomara* gables crowning its facades create an impression of austere and stalwart strength.

The interior of the cathedral, distinguished by an amazing spaciousness and an abundance of air and light—features that are quite unusual for medieval Russian architecture—looks like an immense grand hall with four round pillars.

The walls, vaults, window jambs and pillars of the cathedral are covered with painting

26

26. *The Cathedral of the Dormition. 1475–1479. Architect Aristotle Fioravanti*

27. *The veneration cross at the northern wall of the Cathedral of the Dormition*

28. *The Cathedral of the Dormition. The central part with the iconostasis*

THE CATHEDRAL OF THE DORMITION

It was the noted Italian architect and engineer Aristotle Fioravanti who was commissioned to build the Cathedral of the Dormition, the main church in Russia and the seat of the Russian Orthodox Church. Its construction, carried out on the site of the first stone Cathedral of the Dormition (1326–1327), which had by then become dilapidated, was completed in 1479.

"As if made of one stone" is how the chronicler accurately and vividly described his

27

that is reminiscent of a luxurious particoloured carpet of warm red and brown tones. The fresco compositions dating from the 15th–17th centuries form a continuous story full of profound meaning. The wall paintings were more than once renovated and painted over. In the 1960s, they were restored to their original appearance.

The Cathedral of the Dormition initially served as the burial place of metropolitans

28 ▷

29. *The Cathedral*
of the Dormition.
The interior

32

32

30. *The Icon of the Mother of God "Hodegetria." 12th–14th centuries*

31. *The tent for keeping sacred objects with a reliquary containing the relics of Patriarch Ghermoghen*

32. *The royal seat (Monomakh's Throne). 1551. Moscow*

and patriarchs who were heads of the Russian Orthodox Church. Situated in the Side Chapel of Sts. Peter and Paul are the tombs of Metropolitan Pyotr (d. 1326) and his successor, Feognost (d. 1353). The other tombs are situated along the perimeter of the cathedral walls. An openwork tent cast of bronze by the skilful craftsman Dmitry Sverchkov in 1624 houses a reliquary containing the relics of Patriarch Ghermoghen, who valiantly resisted the Polish invaders in the early 17th century.

The cathedral boasts an exceedingly rich collection of 12th to 17th century Russian icons, including St. George the Victorious (late 11th-early 12th centuries), the Icon of the Saviour "The Golden Hair" (early 13th century), the Icon of the Saviour "The Fiery Eye" and the "Oplechny" (i.e., showing Him to the shoulders) Image of the Saviour (both dating from the mid-14th century), The Apos-

34

33. *Paintings in the central apse*

34. *Fresco composition Akathistos to the Mother of God from the Akathistos Side Chapel of the Cathedral of the Dormition. Late 15th-early 16th centuries*

35.
The Side Chapel of Sts. Peter and Paul with the tomb of Metropolitan Pyotr

◁ 33

35

36

tles Sts. Peter and Paul and St. Pyotr, Metropolitan of Moscow and All Russia, with Scenes from His Life (both dating from the late 14th-early 15th centuries), the cathedral's dedication icon The Dormition (Falling-asleep) of the Mother of God, and many others.

The cathedral was for centuries decorated by the finest painters, jewellers, carvers and embroiderers. One of the legendary relics of the Cathedral of the Dormition is the royal seat of Tsar Ivan the Terrible, known as Monomakh's Throne, made in 1551. The throne is lavishly decorated with exquisite relief carving and is topped with a festive-looking canopy adorned with ornamental arched friezes, *kokoshniki* (decorative elements reminiscent of traditional Russian women's headdress of the same name. *—Tr.*), enormous flowers and vessels. The throne takes its name from the compositions in low relief decorating three sides of its base that depict the legend of acquisition by Grand Duke Vladimir Monomakh of Kiev, who was the grandson of Byzantine emperor Constantine Monomachus (hence his name), of royal regalia —a gold cap and barmy, a kind of a necklace made of gold and jewels and worn on a broad collar—from Emperor Alexius Comnenus of Byzantium, illustrating the thesis of the Moscow sovereigns' succession to power from the Byzantine emperors through the Kievan and Vladimir-Suzdalian grand dukes.

Of particular interest among the cathedral's chandeliers is its huge central chandelier, *The Harvest*, which, according to tradition, was cast from silver retrieved by the Russian troops from the retreating Napoleonic army in 1812.

The Cathedral of the Dormition was not only Russia's main church but also a place for holding grand ceremonies and solemn acts of national significance. It was here that in the

37

38

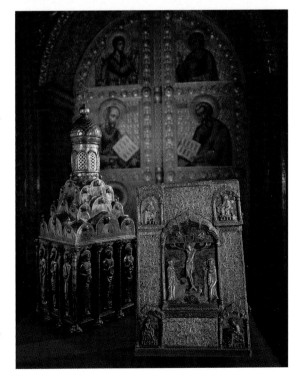

39. *The Gospel. 1499. Moscow. The Lesser Sion (container for holding consecrated Holy Gifts). 1486. Moscow*

39

15th–19th centuries grand dukes were invested and tsars and later emperors were crowned, the ceremony of electing and the rite of consecrating the head of the Russian Orthodox Church were held and the most important national documents were kept.

In 1990, divine services were resumed at the Cathedral of the Dormition. On the days of major church festivals Patriarch Aleksy II of Moscow and All Russia conducts divine services here.

40. *The Cathedral of the Archangel Michael. 1505–1508. Architect Alevisio Novy*

41. *The tombs of Moscow grand dukes Vassily III Ivanovich (d. 1533), Ivan III Vassilyevich (d. 1505) and Vassily II Vassilyevich the Dark (d. 1462)*

42. *The Cathedral of the Archangel Michael. The interior. A view of the western wall from the iconostasis*

THE CATHEDRAL
OF THE ARCHANGEL MICHAEL

In 1505–1508, the Italian architect, Alevisio Novy (the New) built the Cathedral of the Archangel Michael in the south-eastern part of Cathedral Square near the southern slope of Borovitsky Hill. Just as the older cathedral that used to stand on this site it was dedicated to the Archangel Michael, the heavenly patron of Russian warriors. Following the traditions of Russian architecture and preserving the characteristic five-domed shape of the cathedral, the master builder incorporated features of the Venetian palatial architecture of the Renaissance period into the external decor of the building.

The cathedral's wall paintings have a centuries-long history. Between 1652 and 1666, ninety-two masters painted the cathedral anew, having preserved the compositional pattern and subject matter of the 16th-century frescoes. Here one can see compositions depicting numerous deeds of the Archangel

32

43. *The Cathedral of the Archangel Michael. The iconostasis. 1679–1681*

44. *The tomb of Grand Duke Ivan III Vassilyevich of Moscow, the builder of the cathedral (r. 1462–1505).*

45. *Scenes from the Lives of Sts. Varus, Cleopatra and John. Fresco. 1564–1565*

46. *Sculptural portrait of Tsar Ivan IV the Terrible (r. 1533–1584)*

Michael, Biblical scenes, and a kind of a "portrait gallery" of the Kievan, Vladimir-Suzdalian and Moscow grand dukes stressing the idea of the Moscow sovereigns' succession to power.

A special place in the iconostasis completed in 1681 is occupied by the icon The Archangel Michael with Scenes of Angels' Deeds, an outstanding masterpiece of Old Russian icon-painting.

Until the late 17th century the Cathedral of the Archangel Michael served as the family burial place for the Moscow ruling dynasty. In all, there are 45 tombstones, two memorial stones and two reliquaries in the cathedral. The tombs themselves are in the crypt, and there are white-stone tombstones above them decorated with carved floral patterns and inscriptions. In 1906, copper glass-sided shrines were placed over the tombstones. Lying buried in the cathedral are Grand Duke Ivan Kalita, who began the process of gathering the Russian lands around Moscow, and the heroes of the Battle of Kulikovo—Grand Duke Dmitry Donskoi and Prince Vladimir Andreyevich, as well as Grand Duke Ivan III, the builder of the Kremlin. Lying in the sanctuary, behind the iconostasis, is Tsar Ivan the Terrible buried next to his son Ivan, whom

he killed, and at the southeastern pillar, behind an openwork cast bronze grille, is the reliquary of Tsarevich Dmitry, Ivan the Terrible's youngest son, who died in Uglich in 1591, and next to it are the tombs of some of the members of the Romanov dynasty. Beginning with Peter the Great, Russian emperors were buried in the Cathedral of Sts. Peter and Paul in St. Petersburg, and only Emperor Peter II, who died in Moscow in 1730, was buried in the Cathedral of the Archangel Michael.

45

48. *The tombs of grand duchesses (15th–17th centuries) in the crypt of the Cathedral of the Archangel Michael*

46

48

47

47. *Chalice and censer. Tsarina Irina Godunova's donation to the Moscow Kremlin's Cathedral of the Archangel Michael*

49. *The Cathedral
of the Annunciation.
1484–1489*

50. *The Cathedral
of the Annunciation.
A detail of the jasper
floor*

49

THE CATHEDRAL
OF THE ANNUNCIATION

In the southern part of Cathedral Square next
to the Grand Kremlin Palace stands the gold-
en-roofed Cathedral of the Annunciation. In
the second half of the 14th century there
existed a small single-domed stone church on
this spot, which was more than once rebuilt
and overhauled. In 1484–1489, a small three-
domed cathedral with a galleried parvis on a
crypt surrounding it was built in place of the
old church on the orders of Grand Duke Ivan
III. The cathedral was badly damaged by a fire
in 1547. In the course of its reconstruction in
the 1660s–1670s four small single-domed
side chapels were erected upon the corners of
the gallery and another two domes were
added above its central part on its western
side. The cathedral thus became a nine-domed
edifice, and both the domes and the roof were
covered with gilded copper. Its graceful, light
proportions and its rich and varied architec-

50

tural shapes, as well as the picturesque combination of the white colour of its walls and
the gold of its domes lend the Cathedral of
the Annunciation a festive and exquisite look.
Inside the cathedral is not very spacious. At its
western wall is a wide choir loft with a staircase inside the wall leading to it. The cathedral's floor of rare beauty is made of small
blocks of flint intersticed with pieces of agate
and jasper.

51. *The interior
with a detail
of the iconostasis*

51 ▷

52

The cathedral's wall paintings feature a large number of Evangelical scenes combined into several cycles: feasts, the Passions, miracles and parables, and Christ's appearances. Besides, the wall paintings include numerous representations of Biblical prophets and righteous people, apostles, bishops, martyrs, monks, and warriors. Painted inside the domes are the images of Christ the Pantocrator, the Mother of God "The Sign" and the Lord of Sabaoth. Substantial place among the murals in the central part of the Cathedral of the Annunciation is occupied by detailed illustrations to different parts of the text of the Apocalypse. Painted on the pillars above and below the scenes from the Apocalypse are images of saints, above all Byzantine emperors and Russian princes, who were venerated the most in Russia. They include Emperor Constantine of Byzantium and his mother,

all at one time, between 1547 and 1551.

Of much interest are the frescoes in the galleries of the Cathedral of the Annunciation, which served as one of the entrances to the royal palace. They feature a more than 200-figure composition, *The Tree of Jesse*, based on the Biblical family tree of Jesus Christ. The Tree takes up all the vaults and a substantial part of the walls. Here you can also see portraits of Russian princes and classical philosophers.

The iconostasis of the Cathedral of the Annunciation, comprised mainly of 14th and early 15th century icons, is of unique artistic value. Particularly notable is its *Deesis* tier (*Deesis* is a series of icons showing Our Lord enthroned with the Mother of God on His right and St. John the Baptist on His left.— *Tr.*), which is ranked by experts among the

Empress Helen, Princess Olga and her grandson Prince Vladimir Svyatoslavich of Kiev, St. George the Victorious and St. Demetrios of Thessalonica, Princes Boris and Gleb, Vladimir Monomakh, Alexander Nevsky, Ivan Kalita, and others.

The uncovering of early frescoes in the Cathedral of the Annunciation in 1977–1984 made it possible to conclude that the entire ensemble of its wall paintings took shape

53

54

55

56, 57. *Theophanes the Greek (?). The Mother of God. St. John the Baptist. Icons from the Deesis tier of the iconostasis of the Cathedral of the Annunciation. Last quarter of the 14th century. Moscow*

finest monuments of Byzantine art of the second half and end of the 14th century.

In the late 19th century, a six-tiered iconostasis covered on its front side with gilded brass and decorated with an embossed ornament and enamel, which has been preserved to this day, was made for the Cathedral of the Annunciation.

The Cathedral of the Annunciation was the private chapel of the Russian grand dukes

and tsars until 1635, when the Church of the Saviour Behind the Golden Grille was built next to the tsar's private chambers, and it was often mentioned in the chronicles as the church "at the porch in the grand duke's courtyard." The palace cathedral was the place where the sovereigns' family ceremonies such as marriages and baptisms were often held.

The cathedral's crypt (1360s–1416) built of big white-stone blocks has survived to this

56

57

58. *Andrei Rublev (?).*
The Annunciation. The
Nativity of Our Lord Jesus
Christ. Icons from the fes-
tal tier of the iconostasis
of the Cathedral of the
Annunciation. 1st half of
the 15th century

day. It is believed to be the place where the grand dukes' treasury was kept for many years. At present it houses a permanent exhibition, "The Archaeology of the Moscow Kremlin."

In the last few years it has become a tradition to hold divine services in the cathedral on the day of the Feast of the Annunciation, which, as a rule, are conducted by Patriarch Aleksy II of Moscow and All Russia.

59. *"Four-part" icon. Mid-*
16th century

60, 61. *The exhibition*
"The Archaeology of the
Moscow Kremlin" in the
crypt of the Cathedral
of the Annunciation

THE CHURCH OF THE DEPOSITION OF THE VIRGIN'S ROBE

62. *The Church of the Deposition of the Virgin's Robe. 1484–1486*

63. *Metropolitan Iona. Relief representation on the wooden cover of the reliquary. 17th century*

64. *The Church of the Deposition of the Virgin's Robe. The interior*

In 1451, on the day of the Feast of the Deposition of the Virgin's Robe that had begun to be celebrated in Byzantium in its day, a Mongol-Tatar army led by Prince Mazovsha, which had approached Moscow, suddenly lifted the siege of the city and retreated. In memory of the deliverance of Moscow from the Tatars the private chapel of the Russian metropolitans and patriarchs was named the Church of the Deposition of the Virgin's Robe. The church we see today was built by craftsmen from Pskov in 1484-1486 on the site of an older church of the same name destroyed in a fire in 1479.

In the mid-17th century, after the reconstruction by Patriarch Nikon of the Patriarch's Palace, to which a new patriarchal church was added, the Church of the Deposition of the Virgin's Robe adjoining the Terem Palace became one of the private chapels of the tsarinas and tsarevnas.

The small and cosy interior of this graceful single-domed church features the decor of the first half of the 17th century, which has been preserved. The paintings on its walls and pillars illustrate Christian legends and historical events. The main content of the paintings on the two upper tiers of the church's walls is The Life of the Mother of God—a story of Her parents, Her childhood and youth, Her education, and the last days of Her life. The two lower tiers are dedicated to The Akathistos to the Mother of God—a solemn hymn glorifying the Virgin Mary. The church's pillars represent Russian saints—princes and metropolitans. The selection of the representations was linked with the basic political ideas of the period. Higher still are images of the saints with the same names as members of the ruling Romanov dynasty.

The icons in the Church of the Deposition of the Virgin's Robe were painted specially for this church and they form a fully and well-preserved ensemble. The icons of the three upper tiers of its iconostasis and two icons in its lower tier, The Trinity and The Mother of God with Child, were executed by Nazary Istomin, one of the finest icon-painters of the first third of the 17th century.

Today there is a display of late 14th-17th century Russian wooden sculpture in the northern gallery of the church built over its parvis in the 17th century, which includes a number of monumental carved statues of saints, carved icons, crosses and miniature triptychs. The oldest of the exhibits is the sculpture St. George the Victorious (late 14th-early 15th centuries).

central support was built for grand receptions of the top church hierarchs and for holding church councils. In 1763, after a stove for preparing chrism—a mixture of olive oil and balsam used for sacramental anointing—under a carved ornamental wooden canopy was installed in the hall, it became known as the Chrism Chamber.

Since 1963, the Patriarch's Palace has been housing a Museum of 17th Century Russian Life and Applied Art. More than a thousand exhibits on display here give and idea of the aesthetic notions, artistic tastes and customs of Russian society in that period. Here one can see various gold and silver plate made by Russian, West European and Oriental masters; articles of jewellery; rich vestments of church hierarchs; a collection of manuscript and early printed books, including a primer written by Karion Istomin for Tsarevich Alexei, the son of Peter the Great; a

66. *The klobuk (monastic headdress) and cross of Patriarch Filaret. 1st third of the 17th century. Moscow*

67, 69. *The Church of the Twelve Apostles. The iconostasis*

THE PATRIARCH'S PALACE AND THE CHURCH OF THE TWELVE APOSTLES

The three-storied Patriarch's Palace and the adjoining five-domed Church of the Twelve Apostles were the result of reconstruction of the former Metropolitan's Court in the mid-17th-century, in the days of Patriarch Nikon. The palace's chambers are linked by anterooms and passageways. The first floor was used for husbandry purposes and the Patriarch's offices, the second floor housed state apartments and the private chapel, and the third floor contained the Patriarch's private chambers. In the late 17th century, a fourth floor was added on top of the palace.

The main ceremonial hall in the palace was the Groined, or Chrism, Chamber. This hall of impressive dimensions (its floor area is 280 square metres) with a wide vault without

65. *The Patriarch's Palace and the Church of the Twelve Apostles. 1653–1656. Architects Alexei Korolkov and Ivan Semyonov*

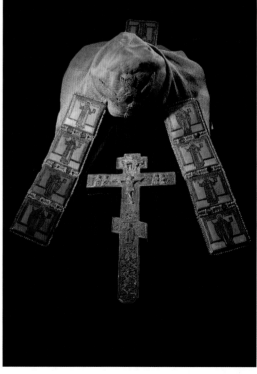

68

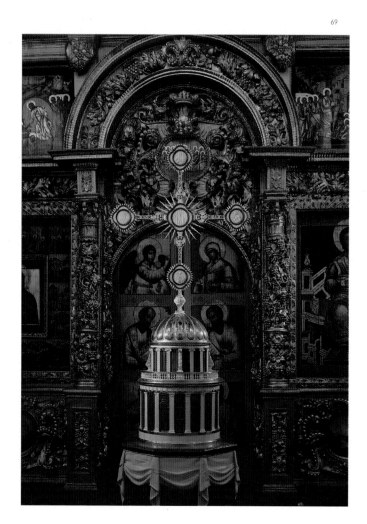

69

70

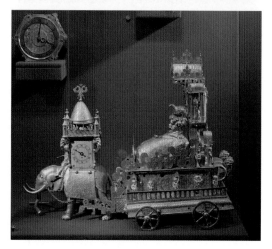

71

68, 70, 71. *The Groined Chamber.*
The display of the Museum of 17th
Century Russian Life and Applied Art

72. *17th-century living room*

collection of bracket clocks and pocket watches; furnishings of a ceremonial royal equipage, and hunting equipment; and a collection of subject and ornamental gold embroidery by Russian needlewomen.

Two small rooms that have retained their old architectural forms introduce the visitor to the interior of a 17th-century dwelling. A stove decorated with polychrome glazed tiles and characteristic samples of furniture—a table, a broad bench, several carved high-backed chairs, a cypress chest decorated with a falconry scene, a German cupboard, and a Dutch wardrobe, which are rare examples of household articles of foreign make that appeared in the everyday life of Moscow dignitaries at the time—help recreate the atmosphere of the period.

A carved portal leads into the Church of the Twelve Apostles. The iconostasis, which was transferred here from the cathedral of the Kremlin's Convent of the Ascension in 1929, features a fine collection of icons of the late 17th and early 18th centuries. On the church's walls is a display of icons by such leading 17th-century Russian painters as Fyodor Rozhnov, Simon Ushakov, Fyodor Zubov, Kirill Ulanov, and Ivan Saltanov.

73

THE ENSEMBLE OF THE IVAN THE GREAT BELL TOWER. THE TSAR BELL. THE TSAR CANNON

Bazhen Ogurtsov, was added to the ensemble. Later on, the Church of the Nativity was converted into a campanile. The campanile and the annex were blown up by the French troops when retreating from Moscow in 1812; subsequently they were restored by the architect Domenico Gilardi after the plans of Ivan Yegotov and L. Ruska.

Altogether there are 21 bells in the bell tower and campanile. The biggest of them, the Dormition Bell, weighs about 70 tons.

Today numerous and varied displays arranged by the Moscow Kremlin State History and Culture Museum-Reserve are held on the first floor of the campanile.

The Tsar Cannon is a remarkable monument of old artillery and a fine example of the craftsmanship of Russian founders. It was cast in bronze by the noted Russian master Andrei Chokhov at Moscow's Cannon Yard in 1586. Few guns in the world can compare with it in size: the cannon has a calibre of 890 mm, is 5.34 metres long and weighs 40 tons, and the outer diameter of its barrel is 1.2 metres.

Originally the cannon was placed near the Lobnoye Mesto in Red Square, defending the approaches to the Spasskaya Tower and in the 18th century it was moved inside the Kremlin. In 1835, the Tsar Cannon was put on a decorative iron gun carriage embellished with cast ornamental patterns. Four decorative iron cannonballs, weighing one ton each, were placed near it.

At the foot of the Ivan the Great Bell Tower stands the Tsar Bell, which has no parallel either in size or in artistic design. It weighs over 200 tons and is 6.14 metres high and 6.6 metres in diameter. The Tsar Bell was cast in the Kremlin in 1733-1735 by the noted Moscow founder Ivan Motorin and his son, Mikhail. During the great fire of 1737 the Tsar Bell still lay in its casting pit. Because of uneven cooling, which resulted from the attempts to extinguish the fire, the red-hot bronze of the bell cracked and a chunk weighing 11.5 tons broke off. After the fire the bell remained in the earth for almost 100 years. It was only in 1836 that it was raised under the supervision of the architect and engineer Auguste Montferrand and put on the granite pedestal on which it still stands today.

Marking the boundary of Cathedral Square on its eastern side is a superb architectural ensemble composed of the Ivan the Great Bell Tower, the Campanile of the Dormition, and the Filaret Annex. The bell tower was built by the architect Bon Fryazin in 1505-1508. In 1600, Tsar Boris Godunov ordered to add another tier on top of the bell tower, which, after it had been completed, reached a height of 81 metres. There is an inscription made in three rows below the gilt dome of the bell tower giving the names of Tsar Boris Godunov and his son Fyodor and also the time that the bell tower was overbuilt. In the mid-16th century the Church of the Resurrection of Christ (Church of the Nativity from 1555) was built next to the bell tower and in 1624 the Filaret Annex with a hip roof, built from the design of

73. *The Ivan the Great Bell Tower. 16th century*

74. *The ensemble of the Ivan the Great Bell Tower. The eastern facade*

75. *The Tsar Bell. 1753*

76. *The Tsar Cannon. 1586*

48

74

THE OFFICE BUILDING

Not far from the Spasskiye Gates is an office building built in the neo-classical style. It stands on the spot where the oldest Moscow cloisters, the Monastery of the Archangel Michael's Miracle at Chonae and the Convent of the Ascension, and also the Lesser Niko-layevsky Palace used to be until 1929.

After the Soviet government moved to Moscow in 1918, the cloisters were closed down and in 1929 the decision was made to pull them down.

The building was built from the design by the architect Ivan Rehrberg in 1932-1934. It was intended for the All-Russia Central Exec-

77, 78. *The Office Building. 1932–1934. Architect Ivan Rehrberg*

77

78

utive Committee Military School, the first military educational establishment for training officers set up after the October 1917 revolution. The building stands near that of the Senate, built by the Russian architect Matvei Kazakov, and harmonises well with it in size, rhythm and colour. In 1938, the Secretariat of the Presidium of the Supreme Soviet of the USSR was moved into the building. Later on, it was redesigned to house the Kremlin Theatre, which existed until 1961. After that the building was reconstructed several times; in particular, a grand Marble Hall intended for use on state occasions was built inside it.

79. *The Office Building.*
The conference hall

80. *The Office Building.*
The interior

THE GRAND KREMLIN PALACE

The Grand Kremlin Palace was built in 1838–1849 (its wing housing the Armoury was completed in 1851) from the design by the architect Konstantin Ton with the participation of Moscow architects F. F. Richter, N. I. Chichagov, V. A. Bakarev, P. A. Gerasimov, painter Fyodor Solntsev, and others. Emperor Nicholas I personally monitored the progress of the construction work and approved each drawing of the design of his Moscow residence.

This unique palatial complex in which structures built over a period of five centuries form a single whole has no parallel in Russian architecture. It consists of a system of buildings situated in a rectangle around an inner courtyard. The facade of the main building (19th century) on its southern side faces the Moskva River; its northern side is the Terem Palace (19th century); part of its eastern side is composed of the ancient Tsarina's Golden Chamber and the Palace of Facets (15th century); and on its western side are the Imperial State Apartments.

The main facade of the palace stretches for 125 metres. The projecting terrace is reminiscent of Old Russian promenades, and the window openings are decorated with carved white-stone platbands with double arches connected by a hanging tie-piece characteristic of 17th-century Russian terem palaces.

Over the central part of the palace rises a rectangular attic with keel arches inside which the figures of double-headed eagles are placed. The attic's dome has a clock with chimes in it and above its roof in the centre there is a flagpole. On the crest of the roof there is an openwork gilt grille.

The Grand Kremlin Palace surpassed all the contemporary palatial structures in monumentality and richness of decor.

In 1932–1934, its splendid Andreyevsky (St. Andrew's) and Alexandrovsky (St. Alexander's) Halls were combined into an austere-looking meeting hall (architect I. A. Ivanov-Schutz) where congresses of the Communist party and sessions of the Supreme Soviets of the USSR and the Russian Federation used to be held. In 1999, the halls were restored to their original splendour.

Today the Grand Kremlin Palace is the place where the President of the Russian Federation holds the most important state receptions. It is here that all major negotiations and the ceremonies of signing key international agreements are held.

This imposing edifice, square in plan, stands on a high crypt. Its main room is a great hall 495 square metres in area. The interior of the hall has a strikingly festive and solemn look. Its groined vaults are supported by a massive central pillar, which is richly decorated with gilded white-stone carving.

The interior decoration of the Palace of Facets was renovated and altered more than once. In the second half of the 16th century its walls were painted with compositions on

82

84

82. *The Palace of Facets. 1487–1491. The main facade. Architects Marco Fryazin and Pietro Antonio Solari*

83

THE PALACE OF FACETS

The struggle for national unification waged by the Moscow grand dukes yielded brilliant results by the end of the 15th century. The year 1480, when the troops of Grand Duke Ivan III of Moscow forced the army of the Golden Horde to retreat, became the year of liberation of Russia from the Mongol-Tatar yoke. Grand Duke Ivan III proclaimed himself the "sovereign of all Russia." To raise the prestige of the young Russian state, construction work that was to be carried on by Russian and foreign master builders was launched in the Kremlin on a grand scale.

Ivan III invited the Italian architects Alevisio and Marco Fryazin and Pietro Antonio Solari for the construction of an immense splendid palace, which was erected in 1487–1508 and which was later on rebuilt more than once. Only the Palace of Facets, the ceremonial throne hall of the old palace, has survived to this day. Its main facade overlooking Cathedral Square is finished in faceted white stone, from which the name derives.

54

83. The Palace
of Facets. The Krasnoye
Porch

84. The portal of the
Palace of Facets

85. The Palace of
Facets. The interior

86. The Parable of
a Just Judge. Painting
on the western wall

87. *Tsar Feodor Ioan-*
novich. Painting on the
southern wall

88. *The Palace*
of Facets. The interior

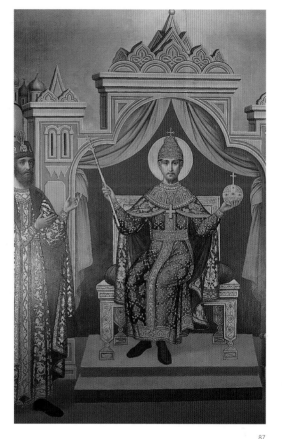

87   88

89. *Grand Duke*
Vladimir Svyatoslavich
with His Sons. Painting
on the eastern wall

90. *Joseph's Feast.*
Painting on the eastern
wall

ecclesiastical and Biblical subjects. On the tsar's orders in 1672, after several fires, the icon-painter Simon Ushakov compiled an accurate and detailed description of the old subjects and texts. In the late 17th century, the old murals were whitewashed and the walls were covered with bright red broadcloth and in the 19th century, with red velvet adorned with representations of double-headed eagles. In 1881, during preparations for the coronation of Emperor Alexander III, it was decided to paint the walls of the Palace of Facets anew, and the job was done by the

Belousov brothers, masters from Palekh (a village renowned for its distinctive paintings), who strictly adhered to the old description.

The subjects of the paintings are united by the main subject, the glorification of the country's centralised power and the affirmation of its historical continuity. Hence the compositions with likenesses of twenty-four Russian rulers from the old Rurikovichi dynasty, including Grand Duke Vladimir of Kiev and his twelve sons, whom he teaches how they should live a righteous life and wisely rule the Old Russian state. In the murals decorating the

56

walls of the Palace of Facets parallels between Old Testament subjects and events of Russian history are to be seen such as the story of the ascension of Tsar Boris Godunov, the next one after Tsar Feodor Ioannovich, to the throne and the story of Joseph from the Old Testament.

The Palace of Facets long remained the largest ceremonial hall in Moscow. The hall of the Palace of Facets was intended for holding various formal functions. Foreign ambassadors were received, major events in the life of the state were celebrated and the sittings of the Boyar Duma (Noblemen's Council) were held in this hall. During grand feasts its floor was covered with carpets and ceremonial precious tableware was placed on the tables. Royal thrones from the Armoury were also installed in this hall.

People entered the Palace of Facets from Cathedral Square by way of the Krasnoye (Beautiful) Porch, a grand entrance with a staircase leading to the Sacred Vestibule, an anteroom at the entrance to the hall, named after the murals on subjects from the Holy Scriptures decorating part of its walls.

In the 1990s, the rooms in the crypt of the Palace of Facets were placed at the disposal of the Moscow Patriarchate of the Russian Orthodox Church and now they house the Kremlin residence of the Patriarch of Moscow and All Russia.

THE TSARINA'S GOLDEN CHAMBER

91. *The Sacred Vestibule*

92. *The white-stone portal on the western wall of the Palace of Facets*

93. *The Tsarina's Golden Chamber. The white-stone portal. 16th century*

The first mention of the Tsarina's Golden Chamber—the Russian tsarinas' reception hall—dates back to 1526. There have also survived mentions of the fact that in 1589, during the reign of Tsar Feodor Ioannovich, his spouse, Irina Godunova, received members of the top Russian and foreign clergy in it. At the time, the painting on its walls was done on a background of gold, from which fact the chamber derived its name.

The wall paintings we can see now date from the early 17th century. In the course of the centuries, the murals were repainted in oil more than once. It was only in the 1970s, after nine years of complicated and intricate work, that restorers succeeded in removing the later layers of painting.

The main subject of the compositions is the triumph of the Christian faith. This underlying idea determined the selection of personages for the paintings. Substantial place is given to the legend of Princess Olga of Kiev, who was the first Russian princess to embrace Christianity and who did much to establish Christianity in Russia.

In the Tsarina's Golden Chamber, Russian tsarinas received congratulations on the days of church feasts and family occasions. It was also here that ceremonies in connection with the weddings of august personages and funeral repasts in memory of deceased tsarinas were

held and distinguished guests were received.

In the 17th century, in connection with the construction upon the vaults of the Tsarina's Golden Chamber of the Church of the Image of the Saviour "Not Made with Hands" (1635) and of the Crucifixion (1681), the vaults were strengthened with crossed arches and additional iron stays, which considerably altered the chamber's interior.

94

95

96

94. *The Tsarina's Golden Chamber. The interior*

95. *The paintings in the Tsarina's Golden Chamber. 17th century. The interior. The eastern wall*

96. *Queen Dinara's Entry into Tabriz. The northern wall*

THE TEREM PALACE

The Terem Palace (the word *terem* means "upper chambers of a palace."—*Tr.*) was built on the orders of Tsar Mikhail Romanov in 1635–1636 by the Russian master builders Bazhen Ogurtsov, Antip Konstantinov, Trefil Sharutin, and Larion Ushakov. The first floor of the palace is formed by a 15th-century crypt, a continuation of the crypt of the Palace of Facets. The Sacred Vestibule allowed access to the Boyar Platform, a terrace on the roof of the crypt, and then an open stairway led upwards onto the roof of the 16th-century Workshop Chambers where, with some space left between the outer edge of their walls and the walls of the new palace, two residential floors of the Terem Palace were built. From the promenade, which was thus formed on the roof of the Workshop Chambers and which came to be known as the Verkhospasskaya Platform (Upper Platform of the Saviour), one could enter the royal staterooms on the fourth floor by way of a grand

97. *The Terem Palace. 1635–1636. Architects Bazhen Ogurtsov, Antip Konstantinov, Trefil Sharutin, and Larion Ushakov*

98. *The Terem Palace. The Gold-Roofed Teremok and the observation turret*

stairway known as the Golden Porch. The fifth floor, the Gold-Roofed Teremok (Small Terem), is surrounded with a promenade on which, adjoining the Teremok on its western side, stands a steeple-roofed observation turret. The palace is crowned with a high hip roof adorned with an openwork metal crest and weather vanes. The picturesque, festive look of the Terem Palace delighted the contemporaries who had a chance to feast their

of the palace combined carving with multi-coloured painting: in examining its portals and platbands, traces of ochre, cinnabar, light-green paint, and gilt were uncovered. The lush carved decor of the terems is supplemented by tiled friezes of the two upper stories.

The Terem Palace was linked by numerous staircases and passageways with the Boyar Platform, the ceremonial Palace of Facets and Tsarina's Golden Chamber, and with the palace

100. *The Terem Palace. The white-stone decor of the facade*

99

99. *The Terem Palace. The decor of the frontispiece and platband of the Throne Chamber's window*

100

eyes on these "very wondrous chambers."

The white-stone portals, platbands and cornices of the Terem Palace are covered all over with exquisite carving. It features braided floral patterns and figures of mythical birds and animals and heraldic double-headed eagles. The double-span windows of the upper stories are adorned with festive-looking arches and hanging tie-pieces that were traditional in the 17th century. At one time, the lush decor

churches. In the second half of the 17th century, the stairway that led from the Boyar Platform to the Terem Palace was decorated with a cast grille adorned with bright painting and gilt. Its exquisite ornamentation in the form of intertwined spirals and fantastic creatures leaves you amazed with the richness of the master's fancy.

In the 19th century, during the construction of the Grand Kremlin Palace, part of the

Boyar Platform was covered with high vaults and converted into the Vladimirsky Hall. The Verkhospasskaya Platform and the Golden Porch also found themselves inside the palace and were altered: two white-stone lions made in 1845 were placed at the foot of the porch. They hold shields with the monogram of Emperor Nicholas I in whose reign the construction work was carried out. Each arch of the porch is adorned with a white-stone tiepiece in the shape of a lion's head holding between its teeth the so-called "apple of silence," a symbol of nondisclosure of the secrets of the royal dwelling it guarded.

The tsar's living quarters in the Terem Palace with low vaulted ceilings and wooden floors consisted of a suite of rooms following one another. The windows are glazed with coloured glass and the broad wooden windowsills are covered with exquisitely patterned carving. In the first room, called the Front Hall or the Refectory, boyars gathered every morning waiting for the tsar to appear. The second room, known as the Duma or Council Chamber, was where the tsar discussed the affairs of

101. *The Terem Palace. Inner passageways and the exit to the upper promenade*

102. *The Terem Palace. The grand entrance. The Krasnoye Porch*

103. *The Throne Chamber of the Terem Palace*

104. *The tiled stove in the Throne Chamber of the Terem Palace*

106

107

state with boyars. The next one in turn was the Throne Room or the Study. Its gold and red wall paintings, gilt emblems of the principalities subordinate to the Russian tsar, and double-headed eagles, the state emblem of Russia, and the bright ornamental pattern of the round tiled stove lend the interior of this room a particularly festive and solemn look. The middle window of this room is decorated on the outside with round carved columns supported by sculptural figures of lions. The last one in the tsar's private suite of rooms is the Royal Bedchamber with a canopied carved wooden bed. It is connected with a small prayer room, in which there are two carved gilt cabinets housing a number of 17th and 18th century icons.

The original interior decoration and wall paintings in the royal chambers have not survived. The wall paintings that have come down to us were executed in 1836 by painter T. Kiselyov to sketches by Fyodor Solntsev, Academician of Painting. The tiled stoves and the few articles of furniture were reconstructed under the supervision of F. F. Richter from 17th-century samples.

105. *The Duma (Council) Chamber of the Terem Palace. 17th century*

106. *The Terem Palace. The Royal Bedchamber*

107. *The Terem Palace. The Front Hall. The vestibule*

65

THE PALACE CHURCHES

The ensemble of the Grand Kremlin Palace includes a group of small churches. In the 17th century there were eleven of them, not counting numerous side chapels and prayer rooms, but only six remained after numerous alterations made in the 18th and 19th centuries.

In 1393-1394, the Church of the Nativity of the Virgin was built on the orders of Grand Duchess Eudoxia, the widow of Dmitry Donskoi. In 1514, the Italian architect Alevisio Novy made use of the existing building, having turned it into the crypt of the building he was erecting. The older structure was set apart for the Church of the Resurrection of Lazarus, which is now one of the oldest architectural monuments in the Kremlin to have survived to this day. The Church of the Nativity of the Virgin acquired its present-day appearance after its reconstruction in 1681-1684; its wall paintings were done in oil under the direction of T. Kiselyov in the mid-19th century.

108. *The domes of the Terem churches*

109. *The Church of the Nativity of the Virgin on the Vestibule. 1393–1394. The interior*

110, 111. *The Church of the Nativity of the Virgin. The Refectory. The interior*

112. *The Nativity of the Virgin with Scenes from Her Life. Icon. 1st half of the 17th century*

113. *The Church of the Resurrection of Christ. The iconostasis. 1678–1679*

114. *The Royal Door of the Church of the Resurrection of Christ. 1678–1679*

In the same period that the Terem Palace was built the same master builders who were erecting it built the Verkhospassky Cathedral (Upper Cathedral of the Saviour) with a Side Chapel of St. John the Forerunner (originally, of St. Ioann of Belgorod), a private chapel of the Russian tsars. Its baroque carved gilt wooden iconostasis that we see now was made in the 18th century. The four icons made in the form of embossed panels and the Royal Door of nielloed silver were produced in the late 18th-early 19th centuries. The collection of icons includes works by the finest royal painters of the second half of the 17th century.

In the second tier of the Terem Palace is the Church of St. Catherine the Great Martyr, built of brick by the English architect John Thaler in

112

113

115. The Verkhospassky
Cathedral. The Royal
Door. 1801

116. The Verkhospassky
Cathedral. The interior

115

116

1627. The interior of the church was decorated in 1847 from the design of D. N. Chichagov and its iconostasis was made to a sketch by Fyodor Solntsev. In 1654, a Church of St. Eudoxia, which was rededicated to the Resurrection of Christ in 1681 and subsequently came to be known as the Church of the Resurrection, was built over the Church of St. Catherine. The main adornment of this church is its multicoloured iconostasis and a carved gilt choir loft. On the orders of Tsar Feodor Alexeyevich, a Church of the Crucifixion, also known as the Church of the Exaltation of the Precious and Life-Giving Cross, was built over the Verkhospassky Cathedral. Its iconostasis, executed by Vassily Poznansky, has no parallel in Russian fine arts: only the faces and hands of the saints in the icons are painted in oil and their garments and the background are made using the appliqué technique, which involves the gluing of pieces of precious fabrics onto a wooden base.

In 1683, four of the private chapels—the Verkhospassky Cathedral and the Churches of the Resurrection, the Crucifixion and St. Catherine—were covered by a common roof, which was adorned with eleven cupolas crowned with openwork gilded crosses that can be clearly seen from Cathedral Square.

117. *The Church of St. Catherine the Great Martyr. The iconostasis. 1844–1846.*

118. *The Church of the Crucifixion. The iconostasis: 19th century. The icons: 1682*

THE HALLS DEDICATED TO ORDERS

The five halls of the Grand Kremlin Palace that are dedicated to orders are a unique phenomenon in Russian architecture. They embody the idea of the eternal memory of the many generations of people who served their Motherland and were awarded its highest orders.

The palace's largest ceremonial hall, the Georgievsky (St. George's) Hall, is dedicated to the Order of Great Martyr St. George the Victorious, the most honourable Russian military decoration, instituted by Empress Catherine the Great in 1769. The hall is devoted to the commemoration of Russian military glory. The solemn, majestic look of its white walls and vaults richly ornamented with stucco mouldings is emphasised by the glitter of its lavishly

119, 120. *The grand staircase of the Grand Kremlin Palace*

120

119

121. *The Georgievsky Hall. The door giving entrance to the Vladimirsky Hall*

122. *The Georgievsky Hall. The interior*

121

72

124

126

125

◁ 123

gilded chandeliers and girandoles and the carved gilt ornamental patterns of its doors. The marble slabs covering the walls and pylons are engraved in gold with the names of units awarded the insignia of the Order of St. George and of servicemen decorated with the Order of St. George or a full set of St. George's Crosses. Rising along the walls are eighteen convoluted columns crowned with marble statues by the sculptor Ivan Vitali. These are allegorical figures with shields showing the emblems of the lands that were incorporated in the Russian state in the 15th-19th centuries.

The Vladimirsky (St. Vladimir's) Hall is dedicated to the Order of St. Vladimir instituted by Catherine the Great in 1782.

123. *The Vladimirsky Hall*

124. *Detail of the dome with stucco moulding*

125. *Detail of the parquet*

126. *The Yekaterininsky Hall*

The walls of the hall, faced with white and pink artificial marble, are made in the shape of arches. They support a tent vault topped with an octagonal dome. Hanging from the skylight on top of the dome is a gilt bronze chandelier. The vault and cornices are ornamented with gilt stucco moulding and round medallions with representations of the insignia of the Order of St. Vladimir and its motto, Benefit, Honour and Glory. The special feature of the layout of the Vladimirsky Hall is that it links together parts of the palace dating from different periods: the doors and staircases on its different sides lead to the 15th-century Palace of Facets, the 16th-century Tsarina's Golden Chamber, the 17th-century Terem Palace, and the 19th-century Georgievsky Hall.

The Yekaterininsky (St. Catherine's) Hall, formerly the throne room of the Russian empresses, is dedicated to the Order of St. Catherine instituted by Peter the Great in 1714. Its carved gilt doors and walls hung with grey watered silk are ornamented with decorative insignia of the order against the background of the order's ribbon bearing its motto, For Love and Motherland.

127 – 129.

The Alexandrovsky Hall

128

129

130. *The Grand Kremlin Palace. The Guests' Annex. The Front Hall*

131. *The Grand Kremlin Palace. The Guests' Annex. The Petrovsky Hall*

130

The Alexandrovsky (St. Alexander's) Hall was named after the Order of St. Alexander Nevsky instituted in 1725. The order's motto is For Toil and Fatherland. The walls of the hall are faced with pink artificial marble and its spherical dome is decorated with representations of the national emblem, the insignias of the order and the emblems of the guberniyas (provinces) and regions of Russia.

The Andreyevsky (St. Andrew's) Hall, the throne hall of the Russian emperors, is dedicated to the Order of St. Andrew the First-Called instituted by Peter the Great in 1698. The walls of the hall are hung with light-blue silk of the colour of the order's ribbon and decorated with the order's insignia.

In 1995-1999, simultaneously with the restoration of the Alexandrovsky and Andreyevsky Halls, reconstruction of a gallery adjoining them and of an annex to the palace

132. *The Grand Kremlin Palace. The Guests' Annex. The Damask Hall*

133. *The Grand Kremlin Palace. The Red Drawing Room*

132

133

built in the 1930s was carried out. The reconstruction work was done by an artistic workshop headed by the painter Ilya Glazunov, and he himself was the author and artistic director of the reconstruction project. The original appearance of the gallery was altered. Its deep crimson walls are divided by columns imitating malachite. In the oval medallions installed in the piers between the windows are portraits of Russian grand princes and emperors members of the Rurikovichi and Romanov dynasties. The gallery is connected with a former service building, which has now been completely rebuilt. The new Petrovsky, Damask, Mantel, Green and Red Halls are intended for holding formal functions.

134. *The State Apartments. The Green Drawing Room*

THE STATE APARTMENTS

Adjoining the Yekaterininsky Hall on its northern side are three rooms—the Grand (Green) Drawing Room, the Grand Bedchamber, and the Grand Dressing Room, which are now a kind of museums of 19th-century Russian decorative and applied art. Porcelain for them was supplied by the Imperial China Works in St. Petersburg, furniture, mainly by the St. Petersburg factories of P. Gambs and A. and K. Turs, and fabrics for upholstering the furniture and for making wall hangings and window draperies, by the Moscow factory of G. G. Sapozhnikov.

The Grand Drawing Room is a spacious room with a vaulted ceiling painted by the Italian painter D. Artari. Its walls are hung with fabric of green and gold and its doors and tables are ornamented with patterned in-

lays of bronze, tortoiseshell, mother-of-pearl and finewood in the boulle style. The decor of the drawing room is supplemented by pieces of bronze and porcelain particularly noteworthy among which is a large china standard lamp in the "Japanese" style with sixty-six lamp holders and several vases for fresh-cut flowers.

The main adornment of the Grand Bedchamber is its columns cut from a monolith of greenish-grey Italian marble and its mantelpiece made of jasper by stonecutters from the Urals.

The walls of the Grand Dressing Room are faced with walnut panels closely fitted and joined together without using a single nail or any glue by cabinet-maker K. Hertz. The shape of the chandelier cut from alabaster at the Moscow workshop of S. Campioni features classical motifs.

135. *The china standard lamp in the "Japanese" style*

136. *The State Apartments. The Red Drawing Room*

135

136

THE PRIVATE CHAMBERS

On the first floor of the Grand Kremlin Palace are the Private Chambers—the imperial family's private apartments. These seven rooms and four small rooms for court attendants on duty form an enfilade passing along the main and western facades of the palace.

In decorating the interiors of the rooms, architects and painters made use of various styles, techniques and decorative elements of classical motifs, the baroque, rococo, and classicism. Each room has an absolutely original look and its decor forms an artistic whole complete in itself. Massive pylons divide the apartments into two parts—a kind of a passageway and the main suite of rooms decorated with festive-looking carving and gilt, wall hangings of rare beauty, splendid furniture, and mantelpieces of various shapes.

137. *The Private Chambers. The Empress's Drawing Room*

138. *The Private Chambers. The clock from the Empress's Study. 1st half of the 19th century. France*

The Private Chambers are lighted by cone-shaped chandeliers of gilt bronze with multi-tiered garlands of crystal pendants and the floors are covered with carpets of carefully selected patterns. The doors of the rooms are made of different varieties of wood and richly decorated with inlaid work and relief woodcarving.

The enfilade opens with the Dining Room. Its decor features the decorative principles of

139

138

classicism and classical motifs, in particular, a combination of artificial marble of light tones in facing its walls, white marble sculptures of mythological characters, Hymen and Leda, and crater-shaped vases adorned with representations of Olympian gods, maenads and satyrs.

In the decor of the Drawing Room (the Empress's Reception Room) with its floral patterns of delicate pastel tones of white, pink and

139. *The Private Chambers. The Drawing Room. The hallway part*

light-blue with gold and gilt furniture of wavy contours the fanciful gracefulness of rococo is to be seen. The room is adorned with a large chandelier decorated with numerous porcelain flowers made at the Imperial China Works and with two porcelain pineapples, one at its top and the other at its bottom, which is why it is called the "chandelier with a pineapple."

The Empress's Study is one of the most festive-looking rooms in the palace. Its white and coloured marble, gilt, bronze, mirrors and the deep dark-crimson damask of its wall hangings and upholstery perfectly harmonise with its boulle furniture. The Empress's Study and the Boudoir are connected by a room in which ladies-in-waiting stayed during their spells of duty. Its walls are faced with walnut

83

140. *The Private Chambers. The Empress's Boudoir*

141. *The Private Chambers. The clock from the Empress's Boudoir. 1st half of the 19th century. France*

panels and decorated with painting on a bright-red background. Of interest here is a vase made of white marble in the shape of the three Graces supporting a flower basket.

The Empress's Boudoir features a silver and pink colour scheme. Its wall hangings, upholstery and window draperies are all made of fabric of the same pattern and colour. The Boudoir's mantel, made by craftsmen from the Yekaterinburg Lapidary Facto-

ry, is faced with pieces of Ural malachite matched in colour and pattern so skilfully that it seems to be cut from a monolith. The mantel is adorned with a bronze clock that has a calendar in the shape of an enamel circle showing the months, the days of the week and the phases of the moon.

The Bedroom is made in blue tones, which, according to the designers, should be reminiscent of the clear night sky. The room has a beautiful mantel of white Carrara marble with a traditional mantel clock and candelabra on the shelf. The Bedroom is separated from the Emperor's Study by a small room with walls hung with green fabric and faced with ash panels.

The Emperor's Study has an austere formal look. Its walls are faced with light ash and its furniture made of Karelian birch is upholstered with black leather.

141

142

143

142, 143. *The Private Chambers. The Emperor's Study*

The furniture in the Emperor's Reception Room is upholstered with doublecloth velvet the colour of which varies depending on the lighting. The fabric was produced at G.G.Sapozhnikov's factory in Moscow.

At present, all these apartments are carefully preserved and are only used on rare occasions in receiving distinguished foreign guests.

THE POTESHNY PALACE.
THE STATE KREMLIN PALACE

The Poteshny Palace, situated near the Kremlin wall between the Troitskaya (Trinity) and Komendantskaya (Commandant's) Towers, was built in 1652 as Boyar I.D.Miloslavsky's chambers. Later on it lapsed to the Crown and was connected by a passageway with the royal palace. In 1672–1677, theatrical performances (amusements) for the royal court were put on at the palace. It was then that it became known as the Poteshny (Amusement) Palace. From 1679, it began to be used as residential quarters for members of the royal family. At the end of the 17th century, it was used to accommodate the Police Office and in 1806 Ivan Yegotov rebuilt it to house the living quarters and office of the commandant of Moscow and added a number of pseudo-Gothic elements to its exterior decor. In 1874–1875 it was reconstructed by N.A.Shokhin, who aimed to restore the building to its original appearance.

In 1960–1961, the last major structure, the State Kremlin Palace, was built in the Kremlin next to the Troitskaya Tower on the site of the old building of the Armoury and several service buildings. The building, square in plan, which contains 800 rooms of different size, is 29 metres high and is sunk 15 metres into the ground. The palace was intended for holding congresses of the Communist Party of the Soviet Union and international conferences. At present, the State Kremlin Palace is mainly used as a place for holding concerts and opera and ballet performances.

144

145

144. *The Poteshny Palace. 1652*

145. *The State Kremlin Palace. 1960–1961. Architects M.V. Posokhin, A.A. Mdoyants and others*

THE ARMOURY

The Armoury is the oldest museum in Russia, a treasury of world significance where artistic values of nine centuries are collected. The collections reflect major stages of the development of the Russian state and the history of Russian and foreign culture.

Over its more than five centuries long existence the functions of the Armoury have changed: in addition to serving as a depository for royal regalia the Armoury sometimes directed the activities of most diverse workshops where gifted craftsmen, commissioned by tsars and church hierarchs, produced a great number of articles used in divine services such as covers for the Gospels and settings for icons, chalices (cups for the wine of Holy Communion), crosses, censers, panagias (pectoral images worn by bishops), etc., as well as articles for use in the royal household—tableware, bowls, bratinas (loving cups), and goblets. These articles, incorporating distinctive

146. *The Armoury building. 1851. Architect Konstantin Ton*

147. *The Armoury. The main entrance hall and the grand staircase*

87

features of national art, amaze you with the craftsmen's rich imagination and great skill.

In the early centuries of the Armoury's existence it had no exhibition halls, showcases and illuminated podiums which are a familiar sight for us now. Its treasures were displayed in a much more spectacular way. Entries that the Armoury's clerks made by their quills in the registers of royal entrances, which have come down to us, contain detailed accounts of what

horsemen clad in fine garments and riding horses whose harnesses were masterpieces of jeweller's art; nowadays, distinguished guests coming to Russia are invited to the halls of the Armoury to feast their eyes on the same finery.

The museum is housed in a building built specially for it from the design by the architect Konstantin Ton in 1851. Its permanent display takes up nine exhibition halls: four on the first and five on the second floor.

148. *The Armoury. 12th-17th century Russian gold plate and silverware. Hall 1*

148

149. *The chain, grivna and two bracelets from the Sudzha treasure-trove. 4th-5th centuries A.D. Northern Black Sea Coast area*

150. *Barmy. From the Ryazan treasure-trove. 12th century*

precious vestments the monarch was clad in, what crown he was wearing on his head and what sceptre he had chosen to be holding in his hand when receiving foreign ambassadors, and the admiration expressed by foreigners in their chronicles for the regalia, gold plate and silverware, and jewels shining on ceremonial weapons is quite similar to the delight which visitors to the Armoury feel in our own day. In the days of old, embassies were greeted by

On display in the first hall of the Armoury is a small yet highly valuable collection of monuments of Byzantine art of the 4th-15th centuries.

Of much interest are articles from a treasure-trove discovered in the upper reaches of the River Sudzha in 1927. These are pieces of jewellery dating from the 4th-5th centuries A.D.: a chain, a *grivna* (an ornament in the shape of a band worn around the neck), two

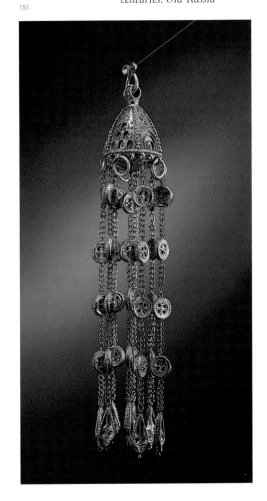

151. *Pendant. 12th-13th centuries. Old Russia*

149
150

152

152. *Stellular kolt (headdress pendant) from the Tula treasure-trove. 12th century. Old Russia*

89

153

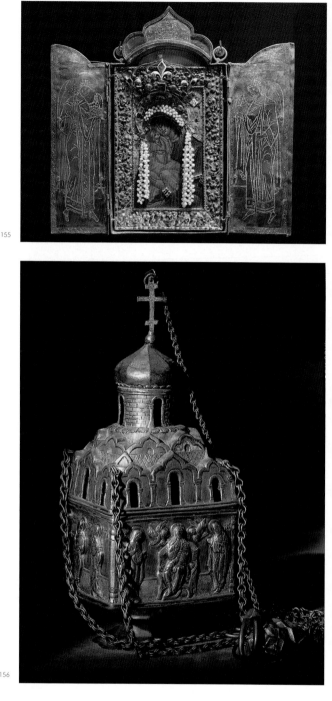

155

154

156

153. *Reliquary. 1589.*
The Moscow Kremlin
workshops

154. *Censer. 1589.*
The Moscow Kremlin
workshops

bracelets, and a gilt silver jug adorned with representations of the nine Muses.

The articles found on the site of Old Ryazan in 1822 are among unique samples of the art of Russian jewellers of the period before the Mongol-Tatar invasion. They leave one amazed with the variety and beauty of lacy filigree patterns and a superb cloisonné technique.

The finest examples of the art of Russian silversmiths include a silver chalice made by craftsmen from the Vladimir-Suzdalian Principality in the 1220s-1230s. Its harmony of shapes, smooth lines, exquisite simplicity and elaborate ornamentation patterns lend a particularly solemn look to this cup for the wine of Holy Communion.

Displayed in two showcases in the first hall are works by 15th-century Moscow craftsmen. The "Morozov" Gospel is an exceedingly rare monument of that period. Presumably, it was made on Metropolitan Foty's commission for the Moscow Kremlin's Cathedral of the Ascension.

In the 16th century, Moscow became a leading centre for the manufacture of gold plate and silverware. Of much artistic value is a group of articles of church plate—a censer, a chalice, a *diskos* (a round plate, elevated on a stand, for the bread of Holy Communion), a star (a cruciform piece of metal which holds the cover over the Eucharistic bread on the diskos), and two platters—made in 1589 on commission from Tsarina Irina Godunova for donating to the Moscow Kremlin's Cathedral of the Archangel Michael. The censer, made in the shape of a single-domed church and ornamented with precious stones and nielloed representations of apostles and saints with the same names as members of the royal family, is decorated particularly lavishly.

The 16th century saw the revival of the enamel technique. One vivid example of this is the setting for an icon of Tsarevich Ivan Ivanovich's heavenly patron, made in 1554. The splendid gold cover of a hand-written Gospel made in 1571—Tsar Ivan the Terrible's donation to the Kremlin's Cathedral of the Annunciation—is also worthy of note. The entire cover is ornamented with a filigree pattern supplemented by enamels of an exquisite, subdued palette.

The Armoury boasts the most complete collection of articles made by 17th-century Russian craftsmen. Gold plate and silverware decorated with precious stones and pearls—ladles, *bratinas* (loving cups), bowls, and cups for drinking wine and strong liquor—helps one form a picture of the splendour of 17th-century court life.

At the turn of the 18th century, Russian and West European cultures began to draw

157. *Reliquary. Byzantium. 11th century*

158. *The setting of the Smolensk Icon of the Mother of God. Late 16th century. Moscow*

157

158

155. *The setting of the Icon of the Mother of God "Eleusa" ("Tenderness"). Moscow. 1st third of the 17th century*

156. *Censer from the Pesnosha Monastery of St. Nicholas the Miracle-Worker. Late 15th century*

closer thanks to the reforms carried out by Peter the Great. The subsequent development of Russian art proceeded along the same lines as West European art. The traditional shapes and purposes of vessels kept changing. Thus, for instance, ancient boat-shaped ladles were no longer used as drinking vessels; now they began to be awarded as a form of distinction.

In the 19th century, major changes took place in the process of making jewellery arti-

surprise Easter eggs which were given as presents on Easter Day. For many years they were made on commission from the imperial family.

The articles of 12th–19th century weaponry which are to be seen here were witnesses to major historical events. The Armoury was a royal treasury and all the samples of Russian, West European and Oriental military, ceremonial and hunting arms and knightly armour that are on display at the museum are richly

159. *West European silverware. 13th–19th centuries*

159

160. *The Gospel cover. 1794. St. Petersburg*

161. *Chalice. 1664. The Moscow Kremlin workshops*

cles. A number of major jewellery producing firms such as those of Fabergé, Sazikov, Khlebnikov, factories of Ovchinnikov, Semyonov and others were founded in Moscow and St. Petersburg. The firm of Peter Carl Fabergé, which produced figurines from semiprecious stones, snuffboxes, powder-boxes, jewellery, etc., became world-famous. The masters of this firm were particularly distinguished from all others for their great skill in making so-called

ornamented using various techniques of artistic metalworking and are inlaid with precious stones, mother-of-pearl and ivory.

The Armoury's display includes a collection of knightly armour, cold steel, and firearms by 15th to 19th century West European master armourers. The central item of the display is a complete set of ceremonial armour that protected both the rider and the horse. Made by Kunz Lochner, the famous ar-

160

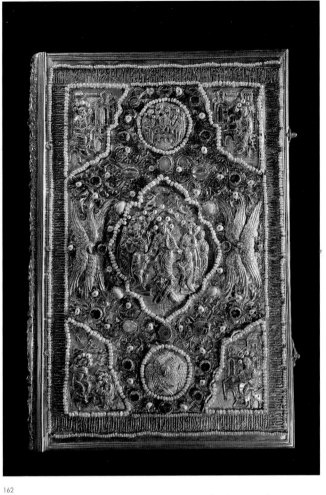

162

161

163

162. *The Gospel.*
1603. Moscow

163. *Tsar Mikhail*
Feodorovich's ladle.
1618. The Moscow
Kremlin workshops

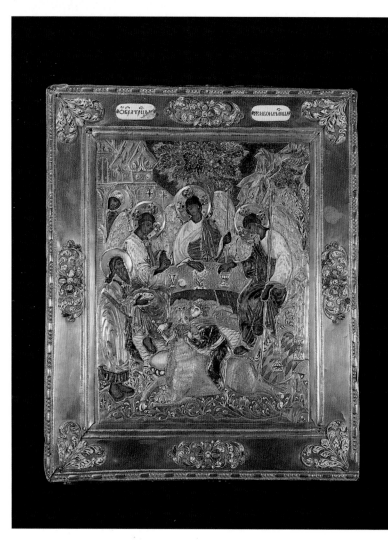

164. *Icon The Holy Trinity in a setting. 1672–1682. The Moscow Kremlin workshops*

165. *Bratina. 2nd quarter of the 17th century*

166. *Sweetmeat platter. 1633–1640. Detail*

167. *Casket. Late 17th century. Solvychegodsk, Russia*

168. *Easter egg with a model of the Alexandrovsky Palace. 1908. St. Petersburg. Fabergé firm*

164

166

165

167

168

170

169

169. *Easter egg "The Tercentenary of the House of Romanov." 1913. St. Petersburg. Fabergé firm*

170. *Clock in the shape of an Easter egg made to look like a vase holding a bouquet of lilies. 1899. St. Petersburg. Fabergé firm*

171. *Easter egg "The Moscow Kremlin." 1904. St. Petersburg. Fabergé firm*

171

mourer from Nuremberg, it was presented by King Stephen Bathory of Poland to Tsar Feodor Ioannovich in 1584.

Predominating in the collection of Oriental weaponry are arms made by 16th-17th century Persian and Turkish armourers such as daggers, sabres, shields, maces, and a helmet. Of the greatest artistic value is the 16th-century shield, made in Persia, which used to belong to Prince F. M. Mstislavsky.

Godunov, a sabre that belonged to Prince Dmitry Pozharsky, and Russian honorary military awards and orders. Most of these articles were made by master armourers from the workshops of the Moscow Kremlin.

A substantial place in the collection is occupied by arms made in the 18th and 19th centuries in Russia's leading centres of arms manufacture such as Tula, St. Petersburg, Sestroretsk, Olonets, and Zlatoust.

172

A major share of the collection of weapons is composed of 12th-17th-century Russian arms and armour. They include an ancient, late 12th-early 13th century helmet that belonged to Prince Yaroslav Vsevolodovich, the father of Alexander Nevsky, Tsar Mikhail Romanov's ceremonial helmet made by Nikita Davydov, the gifted Russian armourer, the famous hauberks and *baidana* (a short-sleeved mail shirt made of rather large rings) of Tsar Boris

Also on display in this hall are arms and trappings that are trophies captured by the Russian army in the Battle of Poltava (1709), which include a hunting set that belonged to King Charles XII of Sweden.

The Armoury also boasts one of the world's richest collections of 13th to 19th century artistic silverware from England, Holland, Denmark, Poland, Sweden, Germany, and France.

173

174
175

173 – 175. *12th–17th
century Russian weapons.
Hall 4*

176. *13th–19th century West European silverware. Hall 5*

177. *Reliquary and pyxis. 13th century. Limoges, France*

The nucleus of the collection is composed of diplomatic and merchants' gifts presented to the Russian sovereigns, which vividly illustrate the history of Russia's political ties and trade relations with other countries and attest to the growth of her international prestige. Aiming to emphasise the importance of the missions of their embassies, European and Oriental monarchs sent the Russian rulers the most valuable silver articles, as well as articles made of natural rare materials and precious stones by the finest masters in the latest style. For the tsar might refuse to accept gifts if he considered them to be below his dignity; for example, this might happen when money and not works of art was presented to him as a gift. According to the etiquette of the period, superiors could make gifts of money to their inferiors but not vice versa.

177

178

178. *Vase. 1st half of the 17th century*

179. *Vessel in the shape of an equestrian figure of King Charles I. Before 1647. Augsburg, Germany*

180. *Collection of 16th—17th century English silverware*

179

180

A collection of articles made by English silversmiths between the mid-16th and the mid-17th centuries occupies a special place in the Armoury's collection of silverware. No other museum of the world has an equally rich and diverse collection of silver plate. In England itself, numerous works of applied art made of silver were made into coins during the bourgeois revolution of 1640—1649.

181. *"Olympian Service." Early 19th century. Sévres, France*

182. *Ice-cream vase from the "Olympian Service"*

In 1917, a grave danger overhung the Armoury's collections and all the valuables of the imperial house, which had been evacuated during the First World War from the arena of war and from Petrograd (the then name of St. Petersburg) and placed for safekeeping behind the high walls of the Kremlin. All the gold and diamond articles from the Hermitage and many other Petrograd museums and suburban royal palaces were stored in sealed boxes in the Armoury and the basements and corridors of the Grand Kremlin Palace. And yet during the few days in October and November 1917 when street fighting went on in Moscow and the Kremlin was surrounded and bombarded with artillery shells, the keepers of the Armoury did not leave their posts and not a single article was lost.

The superb collection of 17th-century Dutch artistic silverware includes about 140 works by masters from Amsterdam, The

183

184

185

Hague, Utrecht and Leiden. These are articles intended to be presented as gifts to the Russian tsar and a large group of articles made specially on the order of merchant Grigory Stroganov.

The most substantial part of the Armoury's collection of silverware is composed of Swedish diplomatic gifts received in the 17th century—a period when Russian-Swedish diplomatic relations were developing most intensively. The collection consists, in the main, of articles brought to Moscow by embassies of Queen Christina and Kings Charles X, Charles XI and Charles XII of Sweden in the period between 1647 and 1699. Most of the articles were produced by German craftsmen from Nuremberg, Augsburg and Hamburg—cities where the art of silversmiths was handed down from generation to generation.

The display also includes diplomatic gifts from Poland and Denmark.

The showcases in this hall look not unlike old-time *postavtsi* (cupboards for holding tableware) in which the Russian tsars' silver-

186. *16th–early 20th century Russian secular garments*

187. *Metropolitan Pyotr's sakkos and crosier. 1322. Old Russia*

188. *Patriarch Nikon's sakkos. 17th century*

189. *Emperor Nicholas II's masquerade costume. 1903. Moscow*

190. *Coronation dress. 1742. Moscow. Belonged to Empress Elizabeth Petrovna*

ware shined, staggering the imagination of foreign guests.

The Armoury boasts an exceedingly rich collection of ancient precious fabrics, artistic embroideries and garments. What makes it particularly valuable is the fact that 14th-15th century Byzantine, 16th–17th century Turkish and Persian and 16th–18th century West European fabrics are represented at the museum not as separate fragments but in the form of well-preserved complete works—secular garments and sacerdotal vestments, tablecloths, curtains, horse covers, etc., which lends it great significance as a collection of articles illustrative of the culture and way of life of the period.

The specimens of 14th–17th century Russian subject and ornamental embroideries are an adornment the museum's collection. The altar cloths, palls, chalice covers, and

191. *The coronation dress-coat of Emperor Nicholas II and the coronation dress of Empress Alexandra Feodorovna*

winding sheets embroidered with coloured silk, gold and silver thread and pearls that are to be seen here are singular examples of "needle paintings." The earliest sample of ornamental embroidery is to be seen on the *sakkos* (bishop's vestment) of Metropolitan Pyotr (1322).

Of great historical and artistic significance is the Armoury's collection of 16th-19th century secular garments. They include Metro-politan Filipp's fur coat covered with homespun cloth (16th century), which has been preserved by some miracle; garments of the Russian tsars and emperors; coronation dresses of the Russian empresses from Catherine I to Alexandra Feodorovna, the wife of Nicholas II, tailored in conformity with the European fashion of their day.

The collection of 13th-19th century royal regalia (crowns, sceptres, thrones, the royal

192. *Collection of 13th–19th century Russian state regalia and court ceremonial articles*

193. *The Cap of Monomakh. Late 13th– early 14th centuries. The Orient. The Cap of Monomakh of the second set. 1682. The Moscow Kremlin workshops*

194. *The throne of Ivan IV the Terrible. 16th century. Western Europe*

193

195

194

196

195. *Tsar Alexei Mikhailovich's diamond throne. 1658. Persia*

196. *Throne. 1604. Persia. Presented by Shah Abbas I of Persia as a gift to Tsar Boris Godunov*

197

200. *The Diamond Cap*
of Tsar Peter Alexeyevich.
1682–1687. The Moscow
Kremlin workshops

197. *The double*
throne of Tsars Ivan
Alexeyevich and Peter
Alexeyevich. 1682–
1684. The Moscow
Kremlin workshops

198

198. *Tsar Alexei*
Mikhailovich's orb and
sceptre. Mid-17th cen-
tury. Istanbul

199. *The Diamond*
Cap of Tsar Ivan Alex-
eyevich. The 1680s.
The Moscow Kremlin
workshops

200

shield and sword, chains, and crosses) and
court ceremonial articles on display at the
museum is truly Russia's national pride.

The symbols of state power—the royal
family relics that the Russian tsars received by
inheritance from their predecessors—
affirmed the continuity and permanence of the
monarchy. They are a kind of a chronicle of the
entire history of the Russian state and witnesses to its most important political events.

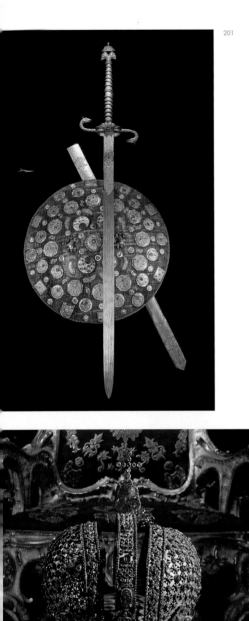

crown, the so-called Grand Attire—a crown, orb and sceptre—made in the 17th century for Tsar Mikhail Feodorovich, the "Cap of Monomakh of the second set" made for the crowning of Peter the Great, the crown of Empress Anna Ioannovna made in 1740 are fine examples of jeweller's art.

Richly ornamented thrones played an important part in royal ceremonies. Ivan the Terrible's ivory throne dating from the 16th century, the oldest throne in the collection,

202. *The crown of Empress Anna Ioannovna.*
1730–1731. St. Petersburg

203. *The throne seat of Empress Elizabeth Petrovna.*
1740-1742. St. Petersburg.
The throne seat of Emperor Paul. 1799–1801.
St. Petersburg

201. *The royal sword and shield. Late 17th century. Moscow*

203

The special significance of the ceremony of crowning tsars and of the coronation of emperors dictated the need to ornament the symbols of power with exceptional splendour, and so quite a few of them have no equal among the world collections in beauty, exquisiteness and the use of rare jewels in adorning them.

The famous Cap of Monomakh, a late 13th-early 14th century crown, the 16th-century Kazan Cap, Tsar Ivan the Terrible's

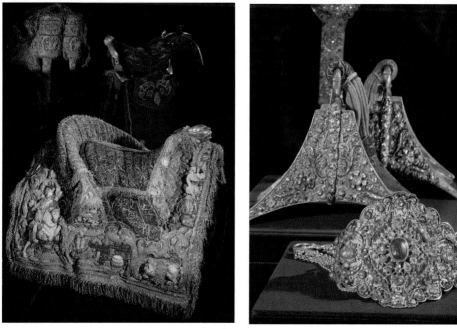

207

206. *Saddle. Mid-17th century. Gdansk, Poland*

207. *Harness ornament and stirrups from a ceremonial harness set for the royal horse. 18th century. Turkey*

204, 205. *Display of the collection of carriages. 16th–18th centuries. Hall 9*

the throne of Tsar Mikhail Feodorovich and the diamond throne of Tsar Alexei Mikhailovich were used during coronation ceremonies until 1896.

The Armoury has one of the world's finest collections of 16th–18th century ceremonial carriages giving the visitor an idea of the development of the art of carriage making in Russia and West European countries. Made by skilful craftsmen from Russia, Germany, England, France and Austria, the carriages are of interest both in terms of their design features and in their decoration. The oldest item in the collection, a heavy coach of English make, was presented to Tsar Boris Godunov by King James I of England in 1603.

The collection of 16th-18th century ceremonial horse attire showing how much importance was attached to the equestrian turnout for the tsar's ceremonial appearances and the

208

208. *Carriage. 1721. Paris*

209. *Carriage body. 1754. Paris, France. Count Kirill Razumovsky's present to Empress Elizabeth Petrovna*

210. *Winter carriage on runners. 1st half of the 18th century. St. Petersburg*

210

ceremony of meeting foreign embassies is truly unique. Ceremonial saddles, bridles and other components of harnesses were made from expensive materials and were richly decorated with gold and precious stones and skilfully ornamented with colourful enamels, embossed patterns in high relief, velvety niello designs, and exquisite engraving. Horse covers were tailored from silk, velvet and brocade and embroidered with pearls and gold and silver threads. Quite often rich harnesses were presented as diplomatic gifts. The Armoury'c collection includes rare sets of harnesses made by Polish, German, Turkish, Persian, Chinese and English craftsmen, and also harnesses from the Caucasus and Central Asia.

211, 216. *Summer carriage and a detail of its ornamentation.*
The 1770s. England.
Count Grigory Orlov's present to Empress Catherine the Great

212, 215. *Carriage and a detail of its ornamentation. 1746. Berlin. Presented by King Frederick II of Prussia as a gift to Empress Elizabeth Petrovna*

211

212

213

213. *Detail of the ornamentation
of the body of a two-seat carriage.
1603. Presented by King James I
of England to Tsar Boris Godunov*

214

215

216

214. *Summer "amusement"
carriage. 1690–1692.
Workshops
of the Moscow Kremlin's
Stable Yard*

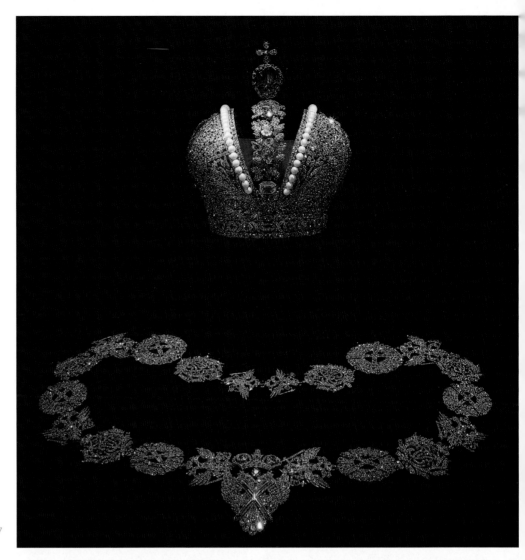

217. *Great Imperial
Crown. 1762.
St. Petersburg*

218. *Orb and sceptre.
1762. St. Petersburg*

217

218

219. *Bracelet. 2nd half of the 19th century*

220. *Star of the Order of St. Andrew the First-Called. 1805–1815*

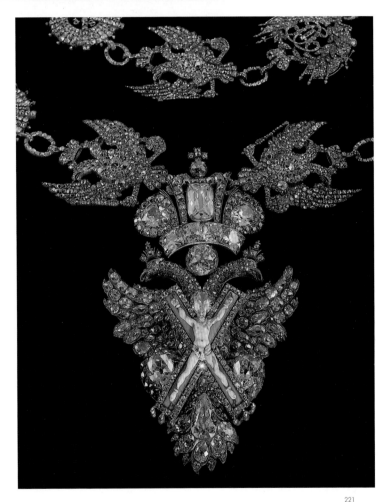

221

THE DIAMOND FUND EXHIBITION

The Diamond Fund Exhibition, opened in the Armoury building in 1967, contains a world-famous collection of rare precious stones, masterpieces of jeweller's art, and platinum and gold nuggets. The treasures of the Diamond Fund are part of the national wealth of the state and since 1922 they have been the responsibility of the State Depository of Valuables (Gokhran) under the Ministry of Finance of the Russian Federation.

The main part of the treasury's collection is composed of ornaments made for the royal house and attributes of imperial power, which were regarded as the property of the Crown, i.e., of the state; hence their name, Crown jewels. It was the signing by Peter the Great in 1719 of a decree which declared regalia (symbols of royal power) objects constituting Russia's glory and pride that marked the beginning of the safekeeping by the state of its

221. *Badge of the Order of St. Andrew the First-Called with a detail of the chain. Late 18th century*

113

Crown jewels. The Diamond Fund's collection of regalia includes the Great and Lesser Imperial Crowns, an orb, a sceptre, the Great Chain with the Cross of the Order of St. Andrew the First-Called, a star of this order, and an agraffe—a clasp that held together the coronation mantle.

All these articles are of great artistic, historical and material value. They were used almost without any alterations during all the

222. *Tourmaline. Presented by King Gustavus III of Sweden as in 1777*

223. *Badge of the Order of the Golden Fleece. Mid-19th century*

224. *Epaulette. 2nd half of the 17th century*

225. *Brooch. 2nd half of the 18th century*

226. *Portebouquet. Ca. 1770*

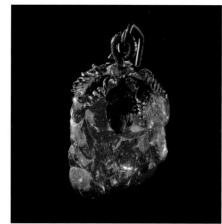

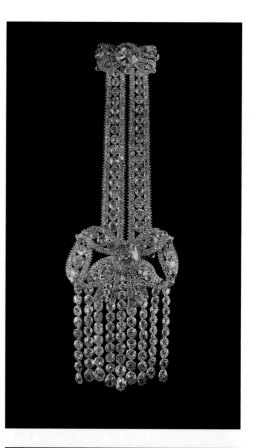

222

223

224

225

coronations, including the coronation of Emperor Nicholas II in 1896.

The Great Imperial Crown, made for the coronation of Empress Catherine the Great in 1762, is the culmination of creative imagination, beauty, splendour and exceptional skill. It is adorned by some 5,000 diamonds forming a superb pattern of laurel and oak branches and a diamond-shaped net. The cold glitter of the diamonds is offset by the dim gleam of

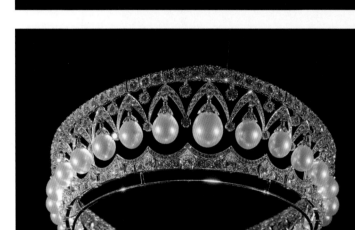

227

228

229

227. *The Grand Bouquet.*
Ca. 1760

228. *Diadem. Ca. 1810*

229. *Diadem Russian*
Beauty, made after
the motifs of ornaments
of the early 19th century.
1987

two rows of pearls. The crown is topped with an immense red gemstone—a nearly 400 carat noble spinel, the world's second in size.

The collection's pride is the world-famous Orlov diamond weighing 189 carats—one of the largest cut diamonds. It adorns the imperial sceptre.

The secular pieces of jewellery which are to be seen here will amaze you with the variety of shapes and combinations of sparkling diamonds with red rubies and spinels, blue sapphires and green emeralds. These are diadems, hairpins, brooches, corsage bouquets, earrings, and dress trimmings. Each article is a masterpiece of unsurpassed artistic value.

The seven so-called "historic" gems include the Shah diamond. What makes it especially valuable is inscriptions with the names of its owners and dates on three of its sides, the earliest of which dates back to 1591. which help to unravel its fascinating history. The gem was brought to Russia in 1829 together with other gifts sent by the Persian shah in atonement for the assassination in Teheran of Russian ambassador Alexander Griboyedov, the outstanding Russian author and diplomat.

115

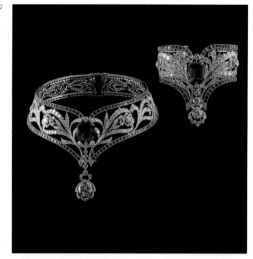

230. *Rose. Brooch. 1970*

231. *Russian Cornfield. Diadem. 1980*

232. *Necklace. 1974. Bracelet. 1977*

233. *Gold nugget The Camel. 1947. The Kolyma River Basin. Weight, 9.288 kg. Fineness, 843° (approx. 20 karats)*

230

231

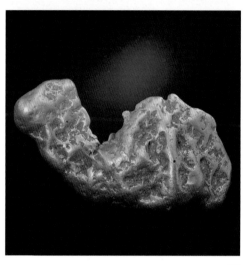

233

Alongside historic jewels on display in the exhibition's showcases are present-day pieces of jewellery made by craftsmen working at the Experimental Laboratory of the Gokhran. Preserving and continuing the finest traditions of Russian jeweller's art, they produce exquisite exhibition pieces adorned with diamonds and coloured precious stones of rare quality.

Only at the Diamond Fund Exhibition can one see so many enormous uncut "named" Yakutian diamonds. They include such giants as the diamonds Alexander Pushkin (370 carats), Free Russia (242 carats), The 26th Congress of the Communist Party of the Soviet Union (342 carats), and others.

Of great value and interest is the collection of precious nuggets—20 platinum and 100 gold nuggets—that has no parallel anywhere in the world.

234, 235. *The Arsenal.*

1786–1795

THE ARSENAL

The building of the Arsenal is situated near the western wall of the Kremlin between the Troitskaya and the Uglovaya Arsenalnaya Towers. Its construction began in 1702, in the reign of Peter the Great, who intended to make it not only a store for arms, but also a museum of Russia's military glory. However, there were long intermissions in its construction and the building was completed only in 1786-1795. In 1812, the French troops blew up the Arsenal during their retreat from Moscow. The blow-up destroyed half of the building. The restoration of the Arsenal was carried out in 1815-1828.

The architectural treatment of the Arsenal is distinguished by monumentality and simplicity. The building, trapeziform in plan, with a large inner courtyard and two gateway arches, is built of brick and decorated with white stone.

In 1960, old Russian and foreign cannons that are of artistic value were placed near the walls of the Arsenal. Prior to that time, they had been near the old building of the Armoury. The best-known among the cannons adorning the facade of the Arsenal are those made by outstanding Russian craftsmen Andrei Chokhov (Troil, 1590), Martyn Osipov (Gamayun, 1690), and others.

Lying next to them are more than 800 cannons of Napoleon's army captured in 1812 by the Russian army following the retreating enemy.

On both sides of the Arsenal's entrance arch are memorial plaques: one commemorating the revolutionary soldiers who died in the Kremlin in 1917 and the other one dedicated to the Soviet servicemen who were killed in the Kremlin during Nazi air raids on Moscow at the beginning of the Great Patriotic War of 1941-1945.

236. *The Senate Palace.*
The grand entrance

237. *The Senate Palace—*
the residence of the President
of the Russian Federation

THE SENATE PALACE—
THE RESIDENCE OF THE PRESIDENT
OF THE RUSSIAN FEDERATION

The building of the Senate is with good reason regarded as a classical example of classicism in the 18th century Russian architecture. Its construction from the design of the architect Matvei Kazakov lasted from 1776 to 1787.

The building was initially intended for housing various offices, the most important among which was the Senate, and also as the place where the nobility of the Moscow Guberniya (Province) would meet. In 1856, it was placed at the disposal of the Ministry of

238. *The Senate*
Palace. The grand
vestibule

239. *The Senate*
Palace. The Yekaterinin-
sky Hall

Justice. After 1918 it housed the Soviet government and Vladimir Lenin's apartment and study. Up to 1993 the building housed the offices of the Council of Ministers of the USSR.

The three parts of the Senate building form a triangle inside which there are three inner courtyards. The buildings of the Senate, the Arsenal and the Armoury (1806–1809) formed a new Senate Square and a kind of a classical ensemble in the Kremlin. In front of the Senate's facade is the grand entrance to the main courtyard. Above the pediment of the building rises the dome of the Oval Hall visually uniting all of its parts.

240

The main room in the Senate is its round white and blue Yekaterininsky (Catherine's) Hall above which rises a 27 metre high dome 24.7 metres in diameter. The hall is adorned with columns and 48 bas-relief portraits of Russian grand dukes and tsars, and also panels depicting major deeds of Empress Catherine the Great. In different periods the hall was known as the White, Yekaterininsky and Sverdlovsky Hall. Congresses of the Communist party were held here and top government awards were presented in this hall.

241

The Oval Hall is decorated in white and green colours. In the years after World War II it was used as the conference hall of the Council of Ministers of the USSR.

After it was decided to make the Senate the official residence of the President of the Russian Federation, extensive reconstruction

242

240. *The banquet hall of the second-floor enfilade of staterooms*

241. *The audience hall of the second-floor enfilade of staterooms*

242. *The National Emblem Hall*

243

243. *The President's library*

244

and restoration work was carried out in the building. After the work was completed, the Senate began to be called the Senate Palace. The imposing decor of its grand halls is combined with the most up-to-date technical equipment making it possible effectively to direct the affairs of the entire vast country right from here. The Yekaterininsky Hall, the main hall of the palace, has once again been ornamented with gilt figures of double-headed eagles and the statues Russia and Justice (sculptor A. A. Bichukov) have been installed in its niches. The hall has been set apart for use on state occasions and for receiving foreign delegations.

The Oval Hall serves as the main office of the country's President. His television addresses are broadcast from this office. Adjoining the reception room is an enfilade of halls; the decoration of each of these halls features its own colour scheme. The third floor is set apart for the President's rest. It contains a chamber theatre, several exhibition halls, and the President's private apartments. Also housed on the third floor is the President's library. In the inner courtyards are two winter gardens inside rotundas that are enclosed in glass.

244. *The winter garden in the southern courtyard of the Senate Palace*

121

RED SQUARE

Red Square is one of the most famous architectural ensembles in Moscow in which civil and church structures are organically blended together to form a single whole.

The first mention of a marketplace, the Torg, near the eastern wall of the Kremlin dates back to 1434. It was the part of the city's area adjacent to the eastern side of the Kremlin wall, which was cleared of rubble after the fire of 1493 and subsequently never built over, that formed the spatial basis of Red Square. Later on the square was enclosed on its southern side by the Cathedral of St. Vassily the Blessed and on its northern side, by the Voskresenskiye (Resurrection) Gates of the Kitaigorod wall.

After the superstructure was added on top of the Spasskaya Tower (1623), the area between the Spasskaya Tower, the Cathedral

245. *Red Square*

mentioned in the chronicles in 1584. The Lobnoye Mesto (in Old Russian this meant a place that can be seen from all round) served as a tribunc for proclaiming the most important royal decrees and announcing death sentences. It was also used for showing the heir apparent to the public when he reached the age of 16.

In the 17th century Red Square became the city's major ceremonial site. It was here that mass religious ceremonies with the participation of the tsar and the patriarch were held. Royal (later on, imperial) processions going to the Kremlin entered the square through the Voskresenskiye Gates and then proceeded to the Spasskiye or Nikolskiye Gates of the Kremlin.

The area in front of the Kremlin wall, however, still remained a marketplace. The first stone shops of the Torg were built on the orders of Tsar Boris Godunov in 1593. They marked the eastern boundary of present-day Red Square. In 1786-1810 the Old Trading Arcade was reconstructed and a New Trading Arcade was built somewhat closer to the Kremlin wall. However, the New Trading Arcade existed only for a short period of time: it collapsed in 1812 when the French troops retreating from Moscow blew up the Arsenal.

The restoration of the Kremlin walls and towers damaged during the occupation of Moscow by the French began in 1816. The moat at the foot of the Kremlin wall was filled in and a lime-tree alley was planted and a boulevard was laid out in its place. After the bartizan in front of the Konstantino-Yeleninskaya Tower was pulled down, the boulevard was continued to the south of the Spasskiye Gates along the slope descending towards the Moskva River, which was named Vassilyevsky (St. Vassily's) Slope.

In 1818, in the presence of Emperor Alexander I and the entire imperial family, the ceremony of unveiling a monument to Kuzma Minin and Prince Dmitry Pozharsky, the leaders of the people's volunteers who drove the Polish invaders out of Moscow in 1612 (sculptor Ivan Martos), was held in Red Square.

In 1883, the imposing State History Museum, built from the design by architect Vladimir Sherwood and engineer A. A. Semyonov, received its first visitors.

In place of the Trading Arcade, which became dilapidated in the second half of the 19th century, a new building of the Upper Trading Arcade (now known as the GUM

of St. Vassily the Blessed and the Lobnoye Mesto began to be called Krasnaya (which in olden days meant "beautiful" but now means "red") Square. By the end of the 17th century, the entire area from the Cathedral of St. Vassily the Blessed to the Voskresenskiye Gates came to be known as Krasnaya Square.

In front of the Spasskiye Gates in the square is a low round stone mound, the Lobnoye Mesto (Place of Execution), which was first

246. *The Voskresenskiye Gates and the Chapel of the Iberian Icon of the Mother of God*

247. *The Cathedral of the Protecting Veil on the Moat (Cathedral of St. Vassily the Blessed). 1555–1561. Monument to Kuzma Minin and Prince Dmitry Pozharsky. 1818*

246

247

State Department Store) was built in 1893 to the design of architect Alexander Pomerantsev and engineer Vladimir Shukhov. This shopping centre has been and remains today the biggest one in Moscow. At the same time, the building of the Middle Trading Arcade was built closer to the Cathedral of St. Vassily the Blessed (1889-1891, architect Roman Klein). After the establishment in Moscow of Soviet power, the funeral of 238 "proletarians who

248

gave their lives for the revolution" was held in Red Square near the Kremlin wall. Their common graves marked the beginning of the shaping up of a revolutionary necropolis.

After the capital of the country was moved to Moscow, military parades and festive demonstrations began to be regularly held in Red Square on May 1 and November 7. Since that time, Red Square became the country's main square.

250

249. *A view of the Lenin Mausoleum from the Spasskaya Tower. Architect Alexei Shchusev*

249

250. *The necropolis by the Kremlin wall*

248. *A view of the Kremlin wall and the Tsarskaya and Spasskaya Towers with the Lobnoye Mesto in the foreground*

In January 1924, right after the death of Vladimir Lenin, the first wooden Lenin Mausoleum (architect Alexei Shchusev) was built in front of the Senatskaya Tower of the Kremlin; a second Mausoleum, which replaced it in 1924, was also built of wood. Finally, in 1930, a granite and marble Mausoleum, the architecture of which ascends to the ancient Egyptian and Persian royal tombs, was built from a new design by Shchusev.

The necropolis by the Kremlin wall has become the honorary burial site for people who did particularly prominent services to the state. Buried in the Kremlin wall itself are persons held in high esteem not only in Russia but worldwide such as the world's first cosmonaut Yuri Gagarin, the pilot Valery Chkalov, the outstanding scientists Igor Kurchatov and Mstislav Keldysh, the spacecraft designer Sergei Korolyov, the writer Maxim Gorky, and a number of prominent military leaders, including the famous marshal Georgy Zhukov. The necropolis is separated from the rest of the square by the Lenin Mausoleum and by stands on both sides of it.

In 1913, a 20 metre high obelisk was put up in the gardens in commemoration of the 300th anniversary of the House of Romanov. In 1918, it was made into a monument to great thinkers and socialist revolutionaries. In 1967, the obelisk was moved further south and on its site a simple and magnificent memorial, the Tomb of the Unknown Soldier, dedicated to the heroic feats performed by the Soviet people during the Great Patriotic War of 1941–1945, was put up. In the centre of the memorial burns the Eternal Flame and next to it are blocks of red porphyry with earth from the hero cities. From 1997, Post No. 1 of the Guard of Honour has been stationed at the Tomb of the Unknown Soldier.

251

252

253

253, 254. *The Tomb of the Unknown Soldier memorial ensemble*

251. *The Alexandrovsky Gardens*   **252.** *The Grotto in the Alexandrovsky Gardens. Architect Osip Beauvais*

THE ALEXANDROVSKY GARDENS

By the 17th century the Neglinnaya River, which barred the way to the Kremlin on its western side, became muddy and shallow and in 1819 it was piped underground beyond the Voskresenskiye Gates of Kitaigorod. In 1819–1823, a park was laid above its cover channel. The park was named the Kremlin Gardens, renamed Alexandrovsky (Alexander's) Gardens in 1856. The entrance to the gardens was from Voskresenskaya Square through large wrought-iron gates. The gardens are adorned with an ornamental grotto with four columns built from the design of Osip Beauvais on an artificial earth bank at the foot of the Srednyaya Arsenalnaya (Middle Arsenal) Tower, which has survived to this day.

254

CONTENTS

THE MOSCOW KREMLIN
An album

Art-Rodnik
Moscow 2001